Android Studio
Game Development

Concepts and Design

J. F. DiMarzio

Apress®

Android Studio Game Development: Concepts and Design

ISBN-13 (pbk): 978-1-4842-1717-7

ISBN-13 (electronic): 978-1-4842-1718-4

Managing Director: Welmoed Spahr
Lead Editor: Steve Anglin
Technical Reviewer: Michael Thomas
Editorial Board: Steve Anglin, Louise Corrigan, James T. DeWolf, Jonathan Gennick,
   Robert Hutchinson, Michelle Lowman, James Markham, Susan McDermott,
   Matthew Moodie, Jeffrey Pepper, Douglas Pundick, Ben Renow-Clarke,
   Gwenan Spearing
Coordinating Editor: Mark Powers
Copy Editor: Sharon Wilkey
Compositor: SPi Global
Indexer: SPi Global
Artist: SPi Global

Distributed to the book trade worldwide by Springer Science+Business Media New York, 233 Spring Street, 6th Floor, New York, NY 10013. Phone 1-800-SPRINGER, fax (201) 348-4505, e-mail orders-ny@springer-sbm.com, or visit www.springeronline.com. Apress Media, LLC is a California LLC and the sole member (owner) is Springer Science + Business Media Finance Inc. (SSBM Finance Inc.). SSBM Finance Inc. is a Delaware corporation.

For information on translations, please e-mail rights@apress.com, or visit www.apress.com.

Apress and friends of ED books may be purchased in bulk for academic, corporate, or promotional use. eBook versions and licenses are also available for most titles. For more information, reference our Special Bulk Sales–eBook Licensing web page at www.apress.com/bulk-sales.

Any source code or other supplementary materials referenced by the author in this text is available to readers at www.apress.com/9781484217177 and at https://github.com/jfdimarzio/AndroidStudioGameDev. For detailed information about how to locate your book's source code, go to www.apress.com/source-code/. Readers can also access source code at SpringerLink in the Supplementary Material section for each chapter.

For Jennifer

Contents at a Glance

Contents

About the Author

J. F. DiMarzio is a seasoned Android developer and author. He began developing games in Basic on the TRS-80 Color Computer II in 1984. Since then, he has worked in the technology departments of companies such as the US Department of Defense and the Walt Disney Company. He has been developing on the Android platform since the beta release of version .03, and he has published two professional applications and one game on the Android Marketplace. DiMarzio is also an accomplished author. Over the last 15 years, he has released 12 books, including *Android: A Programmer's Guide*. His books have been translated into four languages and published worldwide. DiMarzio s writing style is easy to read and understand, which makes the information in the topics that he presents more retainable.

About the Technical Reviewer

Michael Thomas has worked in software development for more than 20 years as an individual contributor, team lead, program manager, and vice president of engineering. Michael has more than 10 years of experience working with mobile devices. His current focus is in the medical sector, using mobile devices to accelerate information transfer between patients and health care providers.

Acknowledgments

The author would like to thank Steve Anglin, Mark Powers, and everyone at Apress for making the process of writing this book an enjoyable one.

Chapter 1

Setting Up Android Studio

Welcome to *Android Studio Game Development*. This book focuses on specific tasks in the process of game development as performed in Android Studio. In this chapter, you are going to install Android Studio and the required Java Development Kit (JDK). By the end of this chapter, you will have a functional Android Studio integrated development environment (IDE) that you can use to develop amazing Android-based games. Let's begin!

Installing the JDK

The first step you want to perform is to download and install the JDK. Because Android applications—including games—are developed in Java, Android Studio needs the JDK to run. The JDK includes many Java tools such as the compiler (javac), the document generator (javadoc), and the key tool (keytool).

> **Note** Although it is true that most Android applications are developed wholly in Java, you can partially develop Android applications and games in C or C++ by using the Android Native Development Kit (NDK). This is an especially popular option with developers who want to share a common library among different builds—for instance, in developing the same game for both Android and iPhone, you could port a single library written in a common language that both systems could interpret natively.

The JDK can be found at www.oracle.com/technetwork/java/javase/downloads/index.html. Figure 1-1 illustrates the JDK download page.

Figure 1-1. The JDK download page

Select the option to download the JDK and you should be directed to the page shown in Figure 1-2.

Figure 1-2. The license agreement page

After you accept the license agreement, the links to download the JDK become active. At this point, you need to download only the JDK and not the Demos or Samples. As always, ensure that you download the correct version of the JDK for your system, if you are running Linux on a 32-bit Intel x86–based instruction chip set, you download jdk-<version>-linux-i586.tar.gz, whereas if you are running 64-bit Windows, you download jdk-<version>-windows-x64.exe.

After you have downloaded the JDK version that is compatible with your system, run the file and install the JDK. I have had luck with simply executing the install package and accepting all defaults.

When your JDK has installed, you will need to set a path environment variable for the JDK on your specific system. The environment variable tells applications where they can find the JDK. Because Android Studio relies on the JDK, it will need to know where to find it on your system. In this case, the variable needs to be named JAVA_HOME.

Note You likely already have the JAVA_HOME environment variable on your system, especially if you have used Java, the Java Software Development Kit (SDK), or the JDK in the past. However, it never hurts to double-check.

On Windows 10, you set this variable by pressing the Win+Break keys. From there, select Advanced System Settings ➤ Environment Variables. Now, create a new environment variable named JAVA_HOME and set to the path of your JDK folder.

With the JDK installed, you can move on to installing Android Studio.

Installing Android Studio

The Android Studio download can be found at http://developer.android.com/sdk/index.html. Figure 1-3 illustrates the Android Studio download page.

Figure 1-3. The Android Developer, Android Studio download page

Once you click the Download Android Studio button, you are presented with a terms and conditions agreement. Activate the download link, seen in Figure 1-4, by accepting the terms and conditions.

Figure 1-4. The terms and conditions page

With the installer downloaded, you can install Android Studio to your system. Execute the installer, and follow the prompts to install Android Studio. I have had great luck in accepting all of the default options presented by the installer.

This installer sets up the Android Studio IDE and sets the default options for how and where your environment will run. It also sets the default size for your emulator.

> **Note**   Although the emulator is a great tool, and it can be used for debugging, I find it much easier and faster to debug using an Android phone (or other Android device). The emulator tends to load run applications slowly. If you are developing business-style software, this may not be an issue for you. However, I have found that for game development, the emulator runs too slow and the GPU emulation is not accurate enough to run a fully emulated game. Therefore, if you have an Android device, put it in Developer mode and use that for debugging (covered later in this book).

Now that Android Studio is installed, it is time to get it updated.

Updating Android Studio

Open Android Studio for the first time. The IDE may look unfamiliar, but let's not worry about that right now; you are going to walk through the IDE in Chapter 3. For now, let's look at the notifications that you may have received.

Chances are, Android Studio has popped up one or more notifications on the right-hand side of the IDE. Figures 1-5 and 1-6 illustrate these notifications.

Figure 1-5. An Android Studio update notification

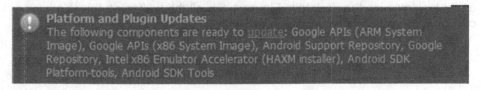

Figure 1-6. An Android Studio SDK update notification

Depending on the timing of your download and of the release of a new version of Android Studio, an update may be available. The good thing about Android Studio updates is that they are fairly painless.

Kick off the update shown in Figure 1-5 by clicking the update link in the notification. Clicking this link brings you back to the Android developer web site, where the required executable is automatically downloaded, as in Figure 1-7.

Figure 1-7. The Android update download page

Once your update is downloaded, and before you execute it, you must close Android Studio. If you do not, you will get a gentle reminder, like that seen in Figure 1-8.

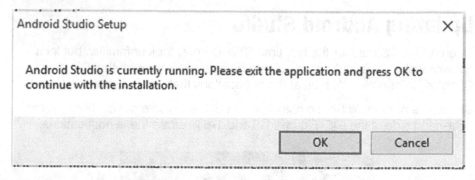

Figure 1-8. A reminder to close Android Studio

The kind of update shown Figure 1-5 is an update to Android Studio as a whole. However, the update in Figure 1-6 is slightly different: this is a component update. This update will change your Android SDK.

> **Note**   This step may apply only if you have an existing version of Android Studio installed on your system. The SDK manager, while it is still an important part of Android Studio, will look slightly different in the latest version of Android Studio. If you installed a new version of Android Studio, feel free to move past this section.

Start the SDK update the same way that you started the update for Android Studio, by clicking the update link in the notification. Now the difference can be seen between the two types of updates.

Android Studio prompts you to complete the update by closing Android Studio, and allowing it to open the Android SDK manager. The Android SDK manager appears as in Figure 1-9.

Name	API	Rev.	Status
☐ Tools			
☑ Android SDK Tools		24.3.4	Update available: rev. 24.4
☑ Android SDK Platform-tools		23	Update available: rev. 23.0.1
☐ Android SDK Build-tools		23.0.1	Not installed
☐ Android SDK Build-tools		22.0.1	Installed
☐ Android SDK Build-tools		21.1.2	Not installed
☐ Android SDK Build-tools		20	Not installed
☐ Android SDK Build-tools		19.1	Not installed
☐ Tools (Preview Channel)			
☐ Android SDK Platform-tools		23.1 rc1	Not installed
☐ Android 6.0 (API 23)			
☐ Documentation for Android SDK	23	1	Installed
☑ SDK Platform	23	1	Not installed
☐ Samples for SDK	23	2	Not installed

Figure 1-9. The Android Studio, Android SDK manager

The Android SDK manager tracks and manages all of the components of the various Android SDKs that are available for, and that you have installed on, your system. For example, if you want to see how your application would function under Android Jelly Bean, you can install that SDK from this screen.

For now, you are just going to install or update the recommend components by clicking the button labeled Install <number> Packages. Clicking this button displays the license agreement window shown in Figure 1-10.

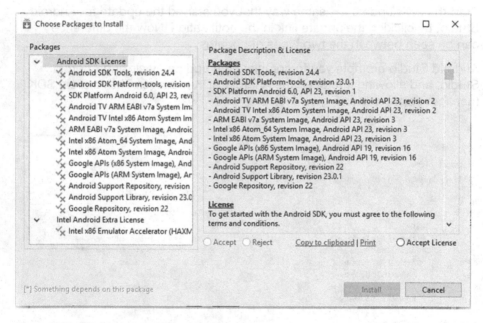

Figure 1-10. The license acceptance window

Accept the license agreements and kick off the update. When the update is completed, restart Android Studio.

With all of your updates applied, you are ready to begin exploring the Android Studio IDE. In the next chapter, you'll discover all the features and tools that make Android Studio a great IDE.

Chapter 2

Creating a New Project

In the preceding chapter, you installed Android Studio. In this chapter, you'll create a new Android project to highlight some of the features of Android Studio. An Android project is the main repository for all the files that make up your application.

Opening Android Studio for the First Time

If this is the first time you have opened Android Studio, the first thing it will try to do is update some functional components. You may end up seeing a window like that in Figure 2-1, before the Android Studio IDE even opens.

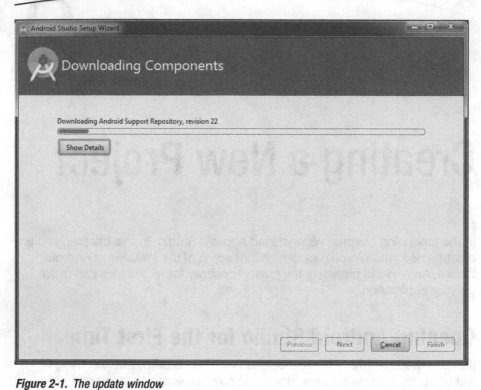

Figure 2-1. The update window

> **Note**   I know that it seems like Android Studio is doing a lot of updating. However, until now, the IDE has not yet run, and it needs to be sure that you have everything you need to run confidently.

After all the updates have downloaded and installed, you are presented with the Android Studio welcome screen, shown in Figure 2-2.

Figure 2-2. The Android Studio welcome screen

In the next section, you'll create a new project to run in Android Studio.

Creating a New Project

The Android Studio welcome screen presents you with a few options. From this window, you can create a new project, open or import an existing project—either from Android Studio or another compatible IDE, or choose configuration settings for Android Studio. Let's select the option labeled Start a New Android Studio Project.

Selecting this option opens the New Project configuration window, shown in Figure 2-3. In this window, you will enter the name and location of your project.

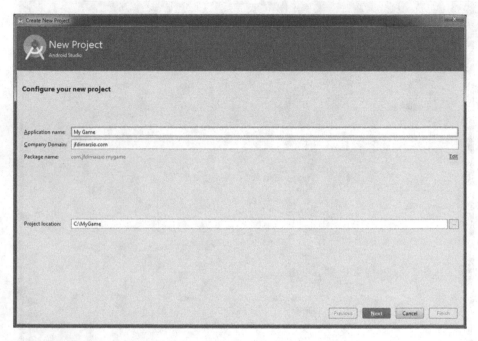

Figure 2-3. *The Android Studio New Project configuration window*

Name your project **My Game** by typing in the Application Name text box. Next, put a name in the Company Domain text box that represents your project. Android Studio tries to automatically name your Java package by using what you enter in the Company Domain text box.

If you want to change the default location where the project will be saved on your system, you can do that in the Project Location text box. Click the Next button to advance to the Target Android Devices window.

The Target Android Devices window, shown in Figure 2-4, lets you select the target on which your application will run. If you will be creating an Android Wear or Android Auto application, you would select that here. Because this project will be used for game development, select the Phone and Tablet check box.

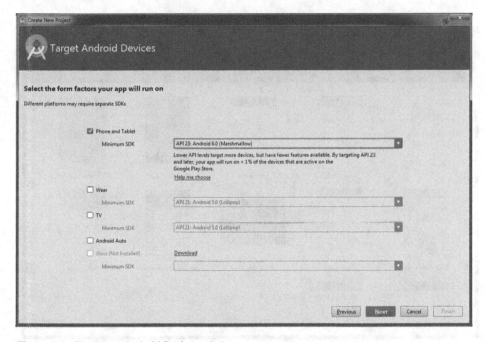

Figure 2-4. The Target Android Devices window

The Minimum SDK drop-down list, configures the lowest OS level that your application will run on. Through your project's configuration, Android allows you to target specific devices. This lets you anticipate, during the development process, what OS level's toolset you can use to create your application.

Android Studio displays for you the installation statistics of each target SDK, and automatically selects for you the minimum SDK with the greatest install base. As of the writing of this book, that SDK is Jelly Bean.

Note   Although Marshmallow is selectable in Figure 2-4, you can see that a project written to run only on this SDK would run on less than 1% of the current install base.

Click Next to move on to the Add an Activity to Mobile window.

In the Add an Activity to Mobile window, shown in Figure 2-5, you select the type of activity you want Android to create for you by default. For the purposes of creating a game project, select Add No Activity and then click Finish.

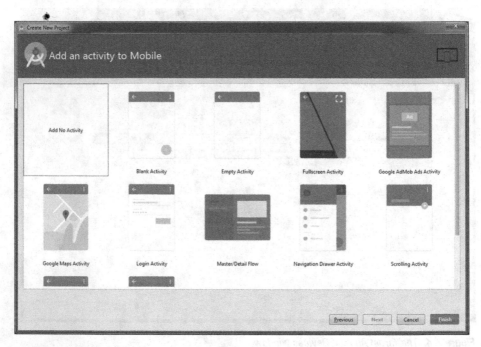

Figure 2-5. The Add an Activity to Mobile window

When Android Studio finishes compiling the options that you selected, the Android Studio IDE will open, as shown in Figure 2-6.

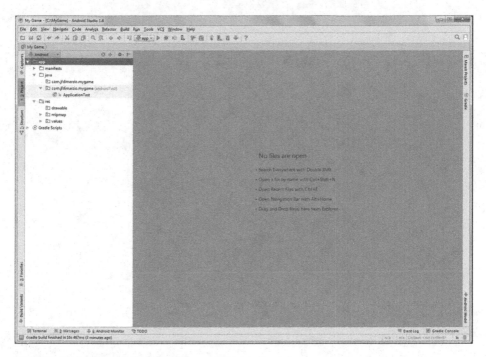

Figure 2-6. The Android Studio IDE

In the next chapter, you'll tour the features of the IDE and learn how to identify the windows used for your development.

Chapter 3

Exploring the IDE

In this chapter, you are going to explore the Android Studio IDE interface. Many tools and features within Android Studio help make the process of developing Android applications easier. This chapter covers the following:

- The layout of Android Studio
- IntelliJ
- Breakpoints

Keep in mind, Android Studio is a massive, full-featured IDE, and I cannot possibly cover all of its amazing features in this mini-book. However, by the end of this chapter, you will be comfortable enough with the major features of Android Studio to make the process of developing games on the Android platform much easier.

Note If you are familiar with any other IDEs, such as Eclipse, NetBeans, or Visual Studio, this chapter will help you put your previous experience to use in Android Studio.

Upon opening Android Studio, you are greeted with a Tip of the Day pop-up, shown in Figure 3-1. Many people immediately uncheck the Show Tips on Startup check box, but you can learn some helpful tricks by giving this pop-up a quick glance when you open Android Studio. I suggest leaving it turned on, at least for a little while.

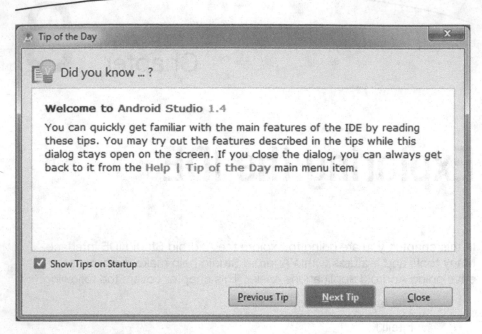

Figure 3-1. The Tip of the Day pop-up

Now, let's take a look at how Android Studio and its features are laid out.

Android Studio Windows

Android Studio is laid out in a series of windows. These windows contain the tools and features that you need to develop your applications. Upon opening Android Studio, you will see an interface that looks similar to that in Figure 3-2.

Figure 3-2. The Android Studio interface

What you see in Figure 3-2 are two of the three main windows that you will use when you develop in Android Studio: the project window and the code editor.

Project Window

The *project window*, shown in Figure 3-3, lists for you all of the projects and their respective files that are present. This gives you an easy way to navigate through your projects.

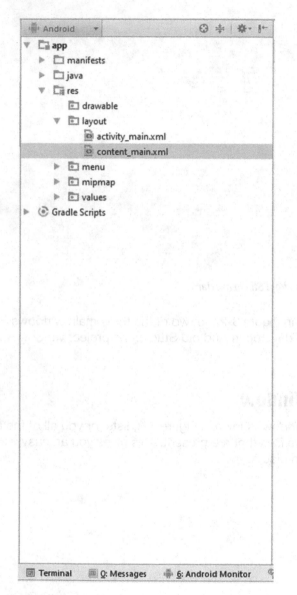

Figure 3-3. The project window

> **Note**   All Android projects, regardless of what the finished application turns out to be, should have the same file structure. Your classes are located in the `src` folder, your XML and resources are located in the `main` folder, and your referenced external libraries are located in the `libs` folder.

To add a new file—be it a class, image, or whatever—you can either right-click the appropriate folder of the project window and choose New ➤ <type of file to be added>, or you can drag an existing file from outside Android Studio and drop it into the desired folder in the project window.

By double-clicking a file in the project window, Android Studio will attempt to open that file in its corresponding editor window. For example, classes and other code files will open in the code editor, layout files will open in the layout editor, and images will open in the image viewer.

Code Editor

The *code editor* is where you will conduct much of your work with Android Studio. This window is where all of the class and XML development is performed. Figure 3-4 illustrates the code editor.

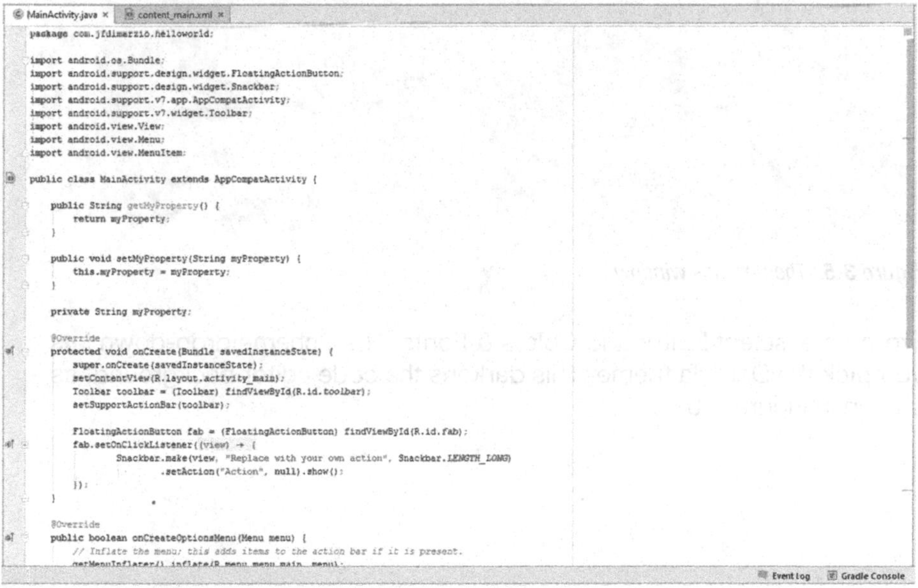

Figure 3-4. The Android Studio code editor

The code within this window is color highlighted to make it easier to read. One change to this window that many developers make is to darken it. Many developers tend to experience headaches and eyestrain from hours of looking at the default colored text on a white background. Changing the code editor background to black can help with this.

Android Studio provides a *editor*theme to help developers change how this window looks. From the File menu, choose Settings. This opens the Settings window shown in Figure 3-5.

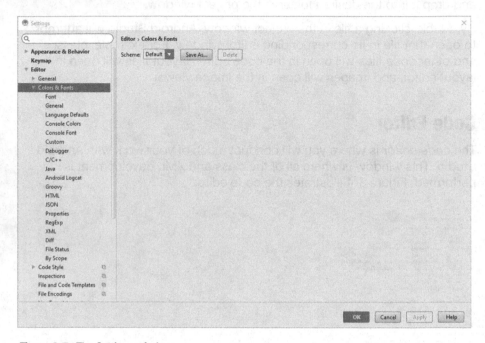

Figure 3-5. The Settings window

From here, select Editor and Colors & Fonts. The Scheme drop-down lets you pick the Darcula theme. This darkens the code editor background, as shown in Figure 3-6.

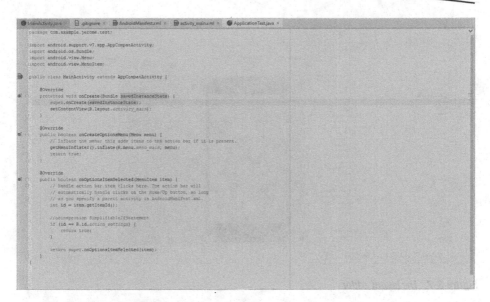

Figure 3-6. The code editor after the Darcula theme

I cover more *editor*about the code window later in this chapter when exploring IntelliJ.

Layout Editor

The *layout editor* is a powerful graphic tool that allows you to create and lay out your Android application screens. Although you might not use this editor often if you are focusing solely on game development, you should still be familiar with its functionality. Figure 3-7 illustrates the layout editor.

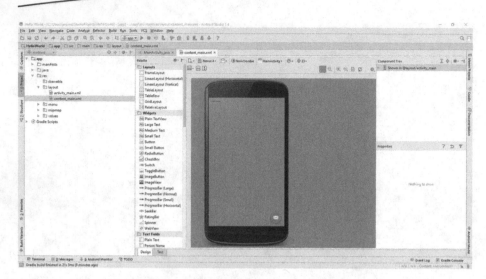

Figure 3-7. The layout editor

Within the layout editor, you can drag and drop widgets onto mock-ups of different Android devices. This allows you to lay out your application's design visually, seeing almost instantly what it will look like on the finished device.

For further tweaking, however, you can always switch the edit to the XML text view by selecting the Text tab at the bottom of the editor. (As shown previously in Figure 3-7, the Text tab is next to the Design tab.)

Now that you have located the two main editors used in Android Studio, it is time to explore one of its most powerful features: IntelliJ integration.

IntelliJ

IntelliJ, or IntelliJ IDEA, is a Java IDEA developed by JetBrains. It has become the de facto IDE for Java development because of its strong feature set. Android Studio is based on the open source community edition of IntelliJ IDEA. This means that many of the features that make IntelliJ IDEA an extraordinary IDE for Java development also make Android Studio an extraordinary IDE for Java development for Android.

Let's go back to the code editor and look at how Android Studio and IntelliJ handle code generation.

Code Generation

IntelliJ has many features in general, and it also has a complete set of tools just for assisting with code generation. The sections that follow cover only those that you are most likely to encounter often as you progress through game development.

> **Note** For a complete list of the features provided by IntelliJ, please visit www.jetbrains.com/idea/help/intellij-idea.html.

Getters and Setters

When creating properties in Java, or in any language really, it can be tedious to have to constantly create your getters and setters. IntelliJ streamlines this process for you. For example, write the following code in your editor:

```
private String myProperty;
```

Place your cursor next to myProperty and press Alt+Insert. This opens an IntelliJ context window. From this window, you can select Getters and Setters, and Android Studio will automatically build your proper Java getter and setter code:

```
public String getMyProperty() {
    return myProperty;
}

public void setMyproperty(String myProperty) {
    this.myProperty = myProperty;
}
```

Autocomplete

Autocomplete is the one features of IntelliJ that is used most often in Android development. Let's say we create a function as shown here:

```
private void DoSomething(String someValue){
    setMyProperty();
}
```

This simple function takes in the String variable someValue. Notice that the function calls setMyProperty(). We know that setMyProperty(), which is a setter created for us by IntelliJ, takes in a String value. Place your cursor inside the parenthesis of setMyProperty() and press Ctrl+Alt+Space. This brings up the IntelliJ autocomplete window, shown in Figure 3-8.

Figure 3-8. The IntelliJ autocomplete window

The great thing to notice about this window is that it not only lists the available String values that you could pass into setMyProperty(), but also sorts them by the ones that it feels you are most likely to use. In this case, someValue—the value being passed into our function—is displayed first.

Breakpoints

Later in this book, I will walk you through debugging your game. However, let's take a quick moment to cover breakpoints. *Breakpoints* are like bookmarks in your code that tell Android Studio where you want to pause execution while you are debugging.

To place a breakpoint, click in the right-hand margin of your code editor, next to the line where you want code execution to pause. A set breakpoint is illustrated in Figure 3-9.

Figure 3-9. A set breakpoint

One of the great things about breakpoints in Android Studio is that you can set them with conditions. If you right-click your breakpoint, you get a context menu that can be expanded to appear as shown in Figure 3-10.

Figure 3-10. The breakpoint context menu

From this window, you can set conditions on your breakpoints. For example, if you have an integer value named myInteger that you set a breakpoint on, you can set a condition to break only if the value of myInteger is greater than 100. Any condition that can be evaluated as true or false can be used as a breakpoint condition.

In the final part of our tour of Android Studio, Chapter 4 concludes with setting up GitHub as your versioning control system.

Chapter 4

GitHub as your VCS

In this chapter you set up a versioning control system (VCS) within Android Studio. This will be the last setup step before approaching the game design concepts.

So what is a versioning control system? At its most base level, a VCS is a repository for storing different versions, or saves, of your code changes. When you work on, for example, a Word document on your computer any changes that you make to that document copy over any previous versions of the document that you had on your system; leaving you with only the most recent set of changes. In software development this is a less than desirable outcome. Many times, you may get days into a change before you realize that there is a better way to do something based on what you had before you saved your changes.

A VCS lets you go back and access any of your previous saves. However, that is not the only great feature of a good VCS. Another feature of a VCS is that it will allow you to collaborate on all of your projects. Friends, colleagues, and trusted members of the general public can be allowed to view and even branch off changes to your base code. This makes the process of creating and working on software a shared experience. If you do not want anyone else to view or change your code, you simply use a private repository – one that only you can access.

While there are many versioning control systems that you could use, the one that we focus on in this book is GitHub.

The first thing you need, to be able to use GitHub, is Git. Git is the version control that GitHub gives you repositories for. Git can be downloaded and installed from http://git-scm.com/download. The Git install wizard is pictured in Figure 4-1.

Figure 4-1. The Git install wizard

While you can generally accept all of the defaults, if you are running on a Windows based system I would suggest selecting the Use Git from the Windows Command Prompt option, as seen in Figure 4-2, when it is presented.

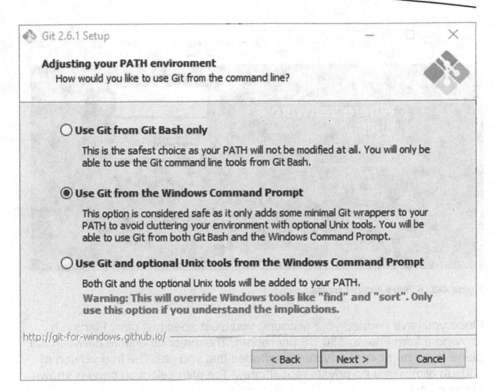

Figure 4-2. Selecting the Use Git from the Windows Command Prompt option

Once Git is installed on your system, you can set up a GitHub account.

Setting up a GitHub Account

Before you can add GitHub as your versioning control system, you must create an account at `http://github.com`. The account creation screen is located on GitHub's home page, as seen is Figure 4-3.

Figure 4-3. GitHub's account creation page

Once you have created your account, you must specify a plan. Plans run
anywhere from Free to $50 US per month. The major difference between the
plans is the number of private repositories that you get. The free version of
GitHub allows you no private repositories. The plan selection page is shown
in Figure 4-4.

Figure 4-4. The GitHub plan selection page

Once you have selected your plan, click on the Finish sign up button at the bottom of the page. That is all there is to setting up the GitHub side of the equation. Now let's set up the Android Studio side.

Setting a VCS in Android Studio

Setting up GitHub as your VCS in Android Studio should be a rather painless procedure. First, click on the File menu and go to Settings. Once in the Settings menu, expand Version Control and select GitHub as seen in Figure 4-5.

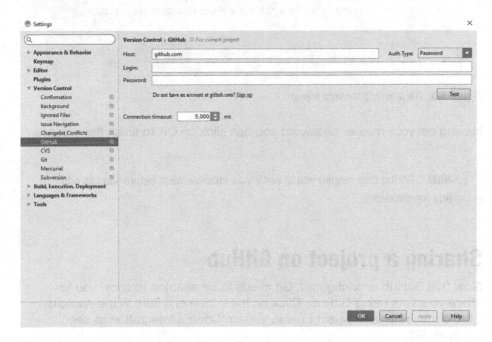

Figure 4-5. Selecting GitHub from the Version Control Settings window

On the right-hand side of the window you are prompted for the GitHub account information that you created in the previous section. Leave the Host as the default – github.com. Provide your Login and Password and click on Apply.

Given that this should be the first time you have added something with a password into Android Studio, you should receive a popup asking you to set a master password – illustrated in Figure 4-6 as follows. This master password is for the password database where all of your account passwords are stored. I would suggest not making this password the same as the one you used on GitHub.

Figure 4-6. The master password popup

Having set your master password you can click on OK to finish the process.

> **Note**   GitHub may require you to verify your email address before you can add any repositories.

Sharing a project on GitHub

Now that GitHub is configured, Git needs to be enabled to allow you to share your Gits using GitHub. Click on the VCS menu item in the Android Studio menu bar and select Enable Version Control Integration as seen is Figure 4-7.

Figure 4-7. Enable Version Control Integration

This opens the Enable Version Control Integration popup that is illustrated in Figure 4-8. Select Git from the dropdown that is on this popup.

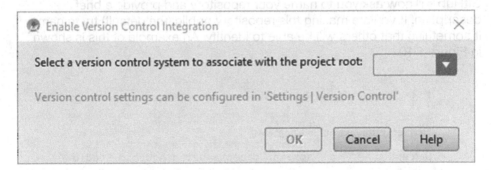

Figure 4-8. The Enable Version Control Integration popup

Note   If after setting Git, you receive an error notification that Android Studio cannot find git.exe, don't fear. Click on the link labeled fix it. This will open the settings for Git. From here you can point Android Studio to the location of your git.exe, which if you accepted the defaults on installation should be Program Files\Git\bin. Once you have pointed Android Studio to your git.exe, you must follow the step to enable version control integration again.

Now you can save your first project out to GitHub. To do this, select VCS from the Android Studio menu bar, and click on Import into Version Control ➤ Share project on GitHub as seen in Figure 4-9.

Figure 4-9. *Share project on GitHub*

GitHub will now ask you to name your repository and provide a brief description. If you are making this repository public (the default) try to name it something that others will be able to identify. An example of this is shown in Figure 4-10.

Figure 4-10. *Naming a GitHub repository*

After you have named your repository you are prompted for which files from your project you wish to add. This will generally be all of the files, however if there is any sensitive information in any of your files keep that in mind before including those files in any public repositories.

Now, if you check your GitHub profile, you should see your new repository. The GitHub that contains the code from this book is located at `https://github.com/jfdimarzio/AndroidStudioGameDev`.

In the next chapter, you are going to learn about game development concepts.

Chapter 5

Intro to Game Development

Developing games on Android has its pros and cons. You should be aware of these pros and cons before you begin. First, Android games are developed in Java, but it is not full Java. Many of the packages that you may have used in past Java development are included in the Android SDK; but some packages that are helpful to game developers, especially 3D game developers, are not included. So not every package that you may have relied on to build previous games will be available to you in Android. This is, of course, assuming you have tried Java game development in some capacity already. If this is your first exposure to game development concepts in any language, you may be at an advantage because you won't have that mental crutch of relying on packages that may not even be available for Android.

With each release of new Android SDKs, more and more packages become available. You will need to be aware of just which packages you have to work with; we'll cover these as they relate to the topics in the chapters.

Another pro, and another con, concern Android's familiarity vs. its lack of power. What Android offers in familiarity and ease of programming, it may lack in speed and power. Most video games, such as those written for PCs or consoles, are developed in low-level languages such as C and even (partially) Assembly. This gives developers the most control over how the code is executed by the processor and the environment in which the code is run. Processors speak very low-level code, and the closer you can get to the native language of the processor, the fewer interpreters you need to jump through to get your game running. Android, although it does offer a limited ability to code at a low level, interprets and threads your Java code through its own execution system. This gives the developer less control over the environment that the game is run in.

This book won't take you through the low-level approaches to game development. Java, especially as it is presented for general Android development, is widely known, easy to use, and can create some fun, rewarding games on its own.

In essence, if you are already an experienced Java developer, your skills will not be lost in translation when applied to Android. If you are not already a seasoned Java developer, do not fear. Java is a great language to start learning on.

Now that you have taken a look at a few pros and cons to Android development, let's discuss the first basic concept of game development: the game engine.

The Game Engine

At the core of every video game is the game engine, and part of that game engine is the game loop. Just as its name suggests, the *game engine* is the code that powers the game, and the *game loop* is a block of code within the game engine that runs repeatedly and executes all of the functions that make up your game.

Every game, regardless of the type of game it is—whether it is a role-playing game (RPG), a first-person shooter, or a platformer—requires a fully featured game engine and game loop to run. The game engine typically runs on its own thread, giving it access to as many resources as possible. The game loop is usually executed from the main activity of the application.

The game engine handles all the grunt work of the game execution: anything from playing the sound effects and background music to rendering the graphics onto the screen. What follows is a partial list of the functions that a typical game engine performs:

- Graphics rendering
- Animation
- Sound
- Collision detection
- Artificial intelligence (AI)
- Physics (noncollision)
- Threading and memory
- Networking
- Command interpreter (I/O)

All games are executed in a code loop. The faster this loop can execute, the better the game will run, the quicker it will react to the player, and the smoother the action will appear on the screen.

The Game Loop

All of the code necessary to build and draw the screens, move the game objects, tally the score, detect the collisions, and validate or invalidate items is executed within the game loop.

A typical game loop can do the following:

- Interpret the commands of an input device
- Track the characters and/or the background to make sure that no one moves to where they should not be able to move
- Test for collisions between objects
- Move the background as needed
- Draw a background
- Draw any number of stationary items
- Calculate the physics of any mobile objects
- Move any weapons/bullets/items that have been repositioned
- Draw weapons/bullets/items
- Move the characters independently
- Draw the characters
- Play sound effects
- Spin off threads for continuous background music
- Track the player's score
- Track and manage networked or multiple players

This may not be a comprehensive list, but it is a fairly good list of all the things that are expected to be done within the game loop.

It is important to refine and optimize all of your game code. The more optimized you can make your loop, the faster it will execute all the calls it needs to make, giving you the best possible gaming experience.

The next chapter covers OpenGL ES, what it means to your game, and what it does.

6

OpenGL ES and Polygons

OpenGL for Embedded Systems (OpenGL ES) is an open source graphics API that is packaged with the Android SDK. Although there is limited support for working with graphics when using core Android calls, it would be extremely difficult—if not impossible—to create an entire game without using OpenGL ES. Core Android graphics calls are slow and clunky, and with few exceptions should not be used for gaming. This is where OpenGL ES comes in.

OpenGL ES has been included with Android, in one form or another, since the very beginning of the platform. In earlier versions of Android, the implementation of OpenGL ES was a limited version of OpenGL ES 1. As Android grew and versions of Android matured, more feature-rich implementations of OpenGL ES were added. Android Jelly Bean thru Marshmallow developers have access to the powerful OpenGL ES 2 for game development.

So what exactly does OpenGL ES do for you, and how does it do it? Let's find out.

Understanding How OpenGL ES Works with Android

Open GL ES communicates with the graphics hardware in a much more direct manner than a core Android call. This means that you are sending data directly to the hardware that is responsible for processing it. A core

Android call would have to go through the core Android processes, threads, and interpreter before getting to the graphics hardware. Games written for the Android platform can achieve an acceptable level of speed and playability only by communicating directly with the graphics processing unit (GPU).

Current versions of Android have the ability to use either OpenGL ES 1 or OpenGL ES 2 calls, and some have the ability to use OpenGL ES 3. There are big differences among the versions, and which one you use plays a role in determining who can run your game.

Although Android has supported OpenGL ES 3 since version 4.3 of Android, it is up to the phone manufacturers to implement the specific hardware that is capable of using OpenGL ES 3. As of the writing of this book, only these phones have hardware compatible with OpenGL ES 3:

- Nexus 7 (2013)
- Nexus 4
- Nexus 5
- Nexus 10
- HTC Butterfly S
- HTC One/One Max
- LG G2
- LG G Pad 8.3
- Samsung Galaxy S4 (Snapdragon version)
- Samsung Galaxy S5
- Samsung Galaxy Note 3
- Samsung Galaxy Note 10.1 (2014 Edition)
- Sony Xperia M
- Sony Xperia Z/ZL
- Sony Xperia Z1
- Sony Xperia Z Ultra
- Sony Xperia Tablet Z

The code in this book, and the code available from this book's GitHub repository, utilizes OpenGL ES 2 to give you the broadest reach in terms of hardware.

The difference in the hardware that determines which handsets can run which versions of OpenGL is in the GPU. Newer devices have GPUs that use shaders. A shader is still a specialized piece of hardware, but it is much more flexible than its predecessor, the fixed function pipeline. OpenGL ES 2 and 3 work with shaders by using a programming language called OpenGL Shading Language (GLSL) to perform any number of programmable tasks.

Using Shaders

A *shader* is a software-implemented helper, written in a shader language, that performs all the functionality that used to be handled by the fixed function hardware. OpenGL ES 2 works with two types of shaders: vertex shaders and fragment shaders.

Vertex Shaders

A *vertex shader* performs functions on vertices such as transformations to the color, position, and texture of the vertex. The shader runs on every vertex passed into it. This means that if you have a shape made from 256 vertices, the vertex shader will run on each one of them.

Vertices can be small or large. However, in all cases, vertices consist of many pixels. The vertex shader works on all the pixels in a single vertex in the same way. All the pixels within a single vertex are treated as a single entity. When the vertex shader is finished, it passes the vertex downstream to the rasterizer, and then on to the fragment shader.

Fragment Shaders

Whereas vertex shaders process data for an entire vertex, *fragment shaders*—sometimes known as pixel shaders—work on each pixel. The fragment shader makes computations for lighting, shading, fog, color, and other things that affect single pixels within a vertex. Processes for gradients and lighting are performed on the pixel level because they can be applied differently across a vertex.

Setting Up Your Game Loop

The preceding chapter briefly discussed the role of a game loop. It is time to set one up.

By the end of this chapter, you should have four new classes in your project: MainActivity, GameView, GameRenderer, and Starfield.

> **Note** If your project does not already have a MainActivity as a result of creating your project in Chapter 2, go ahead and add one (also available from this book's GitHub at https://github.com/jfdimarzio/ AndroidStudioGameDev).

Set up the MainActivity to look like this:

```java
public class MainActivity extends AppCompatActivity {
private GameView myGameView;
    @Override
    protected void onCreate(Bundle savedInstanceState) {
        super.onCreate(savedInstanceState);
        myGameView = new GameView(this);
        setContentView(myGameView);
    }

    @Override
    protected void onPause() {
        super.onPause();
        // The following call pauses the rendering thread.
        // If your OpenGL application is memory intensive,
        // you should consider de-allocating objects that
        // consume significant memory here.
        myGameView.onPause();
    }

    @Override
    protected void onResume() {
        super.onResume();
        // The following call resumes a paused rendering thread.
        // If you de-allocated graphic objects for onPause()
        // this is a good place to re-allocate them.
        myGameView.onResume();
    }
}
```

GameView is an instantiation of the GameView class, which you now need to create. Right-click the package name in the Project view of Android Studio. Typically, your package name is similar to com.<yourname>.<projectname>. Currently, you should see only MainActivity listed under your package. After right-clicking, choose New ➤ Java Class. Name the new class GameView.

The GameView class should extend GlSurfaceView and appear as follows:

```
public class GameView extends GLSurfaceView {

    private final GameRenderer gameRenderer;

    public GameView(Context context) {
        super(context);

        setEGLContextClientVersion(2);

        gameRenderer = new GameRenderer(context);

        setRenderer(gameRenderer);

    }
}
```

Some things to note are that GameRenderer is another class that you will need to create (shortly). It implements an OpenGL ES renderer that will act as the game loop. OpenGL ES renderers are viewed using a GLSurfaceViewer, which is the purpose of the GameView class.

The line setEGLContextClientVersion(2) sets the version of OpenGL ES to version 2.

Let's create the renderer. Once again, right-click your package in the Project window of Android Studio and choose New ➤ Java Class. Name this class GameRenderer.

The GameRenderer should implement GLSurfaceView.Renderer and be set up as follows:

```
public class GameRenderer implements GLSurfaceView.Renderer {

    private static final String TAG = "GameRenderer";
    private Context context;
    public static float[] mMVPMatrix = new float[16];
    public static float[] mProjectionMatrix = new float[16];
    public static float[] mViewMatrix = new float[16];

    private Starfield starfield;
```

```java
public GameRenderer(Context gameContext) {
    context = gameContext;
}

@Override
public void onSurfaceCreated(GL10 unused, EGLConfig config) {
    GLES20.glClearColor(0.0f, 0.0f, 0.0f, 1.0f);

    starfield = new Starfield();

}

@Override
public void onSurfaceChanged(GL10 unused, int width, int height) {
    GLES20.glViewport(0, 0, width, height);

    float ratio = (float) width / height;

    Matrix.frustumM(mProjectionMatrix, 0, -ratio, ratio, -1, 1, 3, 7);

}

@Override
public void onDrawFrame(GL10 unused) {
    float[] matrix = new float[16];

    GLES20.glClear(GLES20.GL_COLOR_BUFFER_BIT | GLES20.GL_DEPTH_BUFFER_
BIT);

    Matrix.setLookAtM(mViewMatrix, 0, 0, 0, -3, 0f, 0f, 0f, 0f, 1.0f,
0.0f);

    Matrix.multiplyMM(mMVPMatrix, 0, mProjectionMatrix, 0, mViewMatrix, 0);

    starfield.draw(mMVPMatrix);

}

public static int loadShader(int type, String shaderCode){

    int shader = GLES20.glCreateShader(type);

    GLES20.glShaderSource(shader, shaderCode);
    GLES20.glCompileShader(shader);

    return shader;
}
```

```
public static void checkGlError(String glOperation) {
    int error;
    while ((error = GLES20.glGetError()) != GLES20.GL_NO_ERROR) {
        Log.e(TAG, glOperation + ": glError " + error);
        throw new RuntimeException(glOperation + ": glError " + error);
    }
}

}
```

Right away you can see that this class instantiates a Starfield class, the fourth and final class that needs to be set up. However, before setting that class up, there is a lot going on in GameRenderer.

The onDrawFrame() is your game loop. OpenGL calls onDrawFrame() in a loop, so it can serve as the central area for all of your matrix transformations. This is where the objects on the screen are created, moved, destroyed, and tested for collisions.

Right now, the onDrawFrame() clears the screen by using the glClear() call, and sets the camera and the initial matrix by using Matrix.setLookAtM (mViewMatrix, 0, 0, 0, -3, 0f, 0f, 0f, 0f, 1.0f, 0.0f) and Matrix. multiplyMM(mMVPMatrix, 0, mProjectionMatrix, 0, mViewMatrix, 0), and calls the method to draw the Starfield object.

Add a new class to your package and name it Starfield. This class should be set up as follows:

```
public class Starfield {

    static float squareCoords[] = {
            -1f,  1f, 0.0f,    // top left
            -1f, -1f, 0.0f,    // bottom left
             1f, -1f, 0.0f,    // bottom right
             1f,  1f, 0.0f };  // top right

    private final short drawOrder[] = { 0, 1, 2, 0, 2, 3 };

    private final String vertexShaderCode =
            "uniform mat4 uMVPMatrix;" +
            "attribute vec4 vPosition;" +
            "attribute vec2 TexCoordIn;" +
            "varying vec2 TexCoordOut;" +
            "void main() {" +
            " gl_Position = uMVPMatrix * vPosition;" +
            " TexCoordOut = TexCoordIn;" +
            "}";
```

```java
private final String fragmentShaderCode =
        "precision mediump float;" +
        "uniform vec4 vColor;" +
        "uniform sampler2D TexCoordIn;" +
        "varying vec2 TexCoordOut;" +
        "void main() {" +
        " gl_FragColor = texture2D(TexCoordIn, vec2(TexCoordOut.x
        ,TexCoordOut.y));" +
        "}";
private float texture[] = {
        -1f, 1f,
        -1f, -1f,
        1f, -1f,
        1f, 1f,
};

private final FloatBuffer vertexBuffer;
private final ShortBuffer drawListBuffer;
private final int mProgram;
private int mPositionHandle;
private int mColorHandle;
private int mMVPMatrixHandle;

static final int COORDS_PER_VERTEX = 3;
private final int vertexStride = COORDS_PER_VERTEX * 4;

public Starfield() {
    ByteBuffer bb = ByteBuffer.allocateDirect(squareCoords.length * 4);
    bb.order(ByteOrder.nativeOrder());
    vertexBuffer = bb.asFloatBuffer();
    vertexBuffer.put(squareCoords);
    vertexBuffer.position(0);

    ByteBuffer dlb = ByteBuffer.allocateDirect(drawOrder.length * 2);
    dlb.order(ByteOrder.nativeOrder());
    drawListBuffer = dlb.asShortBuffer();
    drawListBuffer.put(drawOrder);
    drawListBuffer.position(0);

    int vertexShader = GameRenderer.loadShader(GLES20.GL_VERTEX_SHADER,
    vertexShaderCode);
    int fragmentShader = GameRenderer.loadShader(GLES20.GL_FRAGMENT_
    SHADER, fragmentShaderCode);

    mProgram = GLES20.glCreateProgram();
    GLES20.glAttachShader(mProgram, vertexShader);
    GLES20.glAttachShader(mProgram, fragmentShader);
    GLES20.glLinkProgram(mProgram);
}
```

```
public void draw(float[] mvpMatrix, float scroll) {

    GLES20.glUseProgram(mProgram);

    mPositionHandle = GLES20.glGetAttribLocation(mProgram, "vPosition");

    GLES20.glEnableVertexAttribArray(mPositionHandle);

    GLES20.glVertexAttribPointer(mPositionHandle, COORDS_PER_VERTEX,
            GLES20.GL_FLOAT, false,
            vertexStride, vertexBuffer);

    mMVPMatrixHandle = GLES20.glGetUniformLocation(mProgram,
    "uMVPMatrix");
    GameRenderer.checkGlError("glGetUniformLocation");
    GLES20.glUniformMatrix4fv(mMVPMatrixHandle, 1, false, mvpMatrix, 0);
    GameRenderer.checkGlError("glUniformMatrix4fv");
    GLES20.glDrawElements(GLES20.GL_TRIANGLES, drawOrder.length,
    GLES20.GL_UNSIGNED_SHORT, drawListBuffer);

    GLES20.glDisableVertexAttribArray(mPositionHandle);
    }

}
```

The Starfield class creates a square that takes up the full size of the screen. However, right now this square is just an empty framework. In the next chapter, you'll map an image into this square and create a scrolling star field.

Chapter 7

Loading Images and Spritesheets

Android games would not be nearly as interesting without images. We all can remember iconic video game images such as Mario, Steve from Minecraft, and Master Chief. In this chapter, you'll load an image into your game and map it as a texture onto the polygon that you created in the preceding chapter.

The image that you are working with is a star field, illustrated in Figure 7-1.

Figure 7-1. The star field image

Adding the Image to Your Project

Before you can use the image, you need to add it to your project. There are two things that you must confirm when adding an image to your project.

First, the size of the image needs to be a multiple of 2 for OpenGL ES to work with it properly. This means that your image must also be square. The star field in Figure 7-1 is a 512×512 image. I have made it a habit to load all of my images at 512×512. OpenGL ES will work with any image that fits into this parameter, so 32×32 or even 256×256 are all valid.

Second, the Android Studio project window needs to be in Project view, not Android view, to be able to add an image to your project by using drag-and-drop. To confirm this, look at the upper-right corner of your project window; a drop-down control indicates either Android or Project by default. There are other options, but right now you just want to confirm that your window is in Project view.

Now you can add the image to your project.

Expand your project tree to uncover the resources folder res, as shown in Figure 7-2.

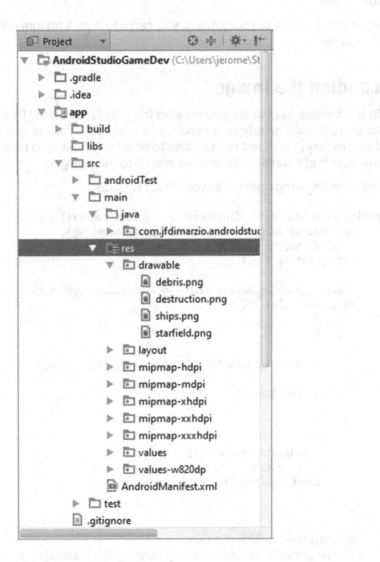

Figure 7-2. The res folder in the project window

Within the resources folder should be a folder named drawable. If that folder does not exist, feel free to create it. All of your images will be placed in the drawable folder. Drag and drop your image from your desktop into this folder.

After the image is in your project, you can use it as a texture and load it into the game.

Loading the Image

In the preceding chapter, you created the Starfield class. This class, in its current state, creates a polygon. In this section, you are going to add a loadTexture() method to this class to allow your image to be loaded into the Starfield class. Then you will map it to the polygon.

Add the following method to your Starfield class:

```
public void loadTexture(int texture, Context context) {
    InputStream imagestream = context.getResources().
    openRawResource(texture);
    Bitmap bitmap = null;

    android.graphics.Matrix flip = new android.graphics.Matrix();
    flip.postScale(-1f, -1f);

    try {

        bitmap = BitmapFactory.decodeStream(imagestream);

    }catch(Exception e){

    }finally {
        try {
            imagestream.close();
            imagestream = null;
        } catch (IOException e) {
        }
    }

    GLES20.glGenTextures(1, textures, 0);
    GLES20.glBindTexture(GLES20.GL_TEXTURE_2D, textures[0]);

    GLES20.glTexParameterf(GLES20.GL_TEXTURE_2D, GLES20.GL_TEXTURE_MIN_
    FILTER, GLES20.GL_NEAREST);
    GLES20.glTexParameterf(GLES20.GL_TEXTURE_2D, GLES20.GL_TEXTURE_MAG_
    FILTER, GLES20.GL_LINEAR);
```

```
GLES20.glTexParameterf(GLES20.GL_TEXTURE_2D,
    GLES20.GL_TEXTURE_WRAP_S, GLES20.GL_REPEAT);
GLES20.glTexParameterf(GLES20.GL_TEXTURE_2D,
    GLES20.GL_TEXTURE_WRAP_T, GLES20.GL_REPEAT);

GLUtils.texImage2D(GLES20.GL_TEXTURE_2D, 0, bitmap, 0);

bitmap.recycle();
}
```

This class takes in an `int` texture, which is going to be a pointer to a resource in the `res/drawable` folder. You will pass this in from the game loop later in this section.

One important thing to note: in the line `GLES20.glTexParameterf(GLES20.GL_TEXTURE_2D, GLES20.GL_TEXTURE_WRAP_S, GLES20.GL_REPEAT)`, the `GL_REPEAT` causes the texture (image) to repeat itself when it is moved on the polygon that you are mapping it to. Think of it as wrapping paper that you are moving across the outside of a box: as you move the paper in any direction, the image will continue to repeat.

To prevent the image from repeating, use `GL_CLAMP_TO_EDGE`. However, in this case, you are using repeating to make the star field appear as though it is scrolling indefinitely.

Next, add some variables to the class to handle the texture operations:

```
private float texture[] = {
    -1f, 1f,
    -1f, -1f,
    1f, -1f,
    1f, 1f,
};

private int[] textures = new int[1];
private final FloatBuffer textureBuffer;
static final int COORDS_PER_TEXTURE = 2;
public static int textureStride = COORDS_PER_TEXTURE * 4;
Add a new texture buffer to the Starfield constructor.
        bb = ByteBuffer.allocateDirect(texture.length * 4);
        bb.order(ByteOrder.nativeOrder());
        textureBuffer = bb.asFloatBuffer();
        textureBuffer.put(texture);
        textureBuffer.position(0);
```

> **Note** The full text of the classes is included at the end of this section, if it seems confusing.

Now, edit the draw() method of Starfield to bind the texture to the polygon. The entire draw() method is show here, because the order of operation is important:

```
public void draw(float[] mvpMatrix) {

    GLES20.glUseProgram(mProgram);

    mPositionHandle = GLES20.glGetAttribLocation(mProgram, "vPosition");

    GLES20.glEnableVertexAttribArray(mPositionHandle);

    int vsTextureCoord = GLES20.glGetAttribLocation(mProgram, "TexCoordIn");

    GLES20.glVertexAttribPointer(mPositionHandle, COORDS_PER_VERTEX,
            GLES20.GL_FLOAT, false,
            vertexStride, vertexBuffer);

    GLES20.glVertexAttribPointer(vsTextureCoord, COORDS_PER_TEXTURE,
            GLES20.GL_FLOAT, false,
            textureStride, textureBuffer);

    GLES20.glEnableVertexAttribArray(vsTextureCoord);

    GLES20.glActiveTexture(GLES20.GL_TEXTURE0);
    GLES20.glBindTexture(GLES20.GL_TEXTURE_2D, textures[0]);
    int fsTexture = GLES20.glGetUniformLocation(mProgram, "TexCoordOut");
    GLES20.glUniform1i(fsTexture, 0);
    mMVPMatrixHandle = GLES20.glGetUniformLocation(mProgram, "uMVPMatrix");
    GameRenderer.checkGlError("glGetUniformLocation");
    GLES20.glUniformMatrix4fv(mMVPMatrixHandle, 1, false, mvpMatrix, 0);
    GameRenderer.checkGlError("glUniformMatrix4fv");
    GLES20.glDrawElements(GLES20.GL_TRIANGLES, drawOrder.length,
    GLES20.GL_UNSIGNED_SHORT, drawListBuffer);

    GLES20.glDisableVertexAttribArray(mPositionHandle);
}
```

In the next section, you will add the code needed to make the image scroll.

Making the Image Scroll

Two changes need to be made to allow your image to scroll. The first is to the fragment shader, and the second is to the draw() method.

The fragment shader is where the actual scrolling of the image will take place. Change your fragment shader to look like this:

```
private final String fragmentShaderCode =
        "precision mediump float;" +
        "uniform vec4 vColor;" +
        "uniform sampler2D TexCoordIn;" +
        "uniform float scroll;" +
        "varying vec2 TexCoordOut;" +
        "void main() {" +
        " gl_FragColor = texture2D(TexCoordIn, " +
        "     vec2(TexCoordOut.x ,TexCoordOut.y + scroll));" +
        "}";
```

Notice that you have added a float variable named scroll, and you are adding the value of that variable to TexCoordOut.y. This effectively moves the image along the y axis. To scroll along the x axis, you would add the value in scroll to TextCoordOut.x.

With the shader logic complete, you need a way to change the scroll value. This is done back in the draw() method:

```
public void draw(float[] mvpMatrix, float scroll) {

    GLES20.glUseProgram(mProgram);

    mPositionHandle = GLES20.glGetAttribLocation(mProgram, "vPosition");

    GLES20.glEnableVertexAttribArray(mPositionHandle);

    int vsTextureCoord = GLES20.glGetAttribLocation(mProgram, "TexCoordIn");

    GLES20.glVertexAttribPointer(mPositionHandle, COORDS_PER_VERTEX,
            GLES20.GL_FLOAT, false,
            vertexStride, vertexBuffer);

    GLES20.glVertexAttribPointer(vsTextureCoord, COORDS_PER_TEXTURE,
            GLES20.GL_FLOAT, false,
            textureStride, textureBuffer);

    GLES20.glEnableVertexAttribArray(vsTextureCoord);

    GLES20.glActiveTexture(GLES20.GL_TEXTURE0);
    GLES20.glBindTexture(GLES20.GL_TEXTURE_2D, textures[0]);
    int fsTexture = GLES20.glGetUniformLocation(mProgram, "TexCoordOut");
    int fsScroll = GLES20.glGetUniformLocation(mProgram, "scroll");
    GLES20.glUniform1i(fsTexture, 0);
```

```
GLES20.glUniform1f(fsScroll, scroll);
mMVPMatrixHandle = GLES20.glGetUniformLocation(mProgram, "uMVPMatrix");
GameRenderer.checkGlError("glGetUniformLocation");
GLES20.glUniformMatrix4fv(mMVPMatrixHandle, 1, false, mvpMatrix, 0);
GameRenderer.checkGlError("glUniformMatrix4fv");
GLES20.glDrawElements(GLES20.GL_TRIANGLES, drawOrder.length,
GLES20.GL_UNSIGNED_SHORT, drawListBuffer);

GLES20.glDisableVertexAttribArray(mPositionHandle);
}
```

You have added a new parameter float scroll to the draw() method. Using glGetUniformLocation(), you can access the scroll variable in the shader and then assign it a new value by using glUniform1f().

The last step is to go back to the GameRenderer class and call Starfield, passing it an image pointer and scroll value.

The image pointer should be passed into the loadTexture() method from onSurfaceCreated():

```
@Override
public void onSurfaceCreated(GL10 unused, EGLConfig config) {
    GLES20.glClearColor(0.0f, 0.0f, 0.0f, 1.0f);

    starfield = new Starfield();

    starfield.loadTexture(R.drawable.starfield, context);

}
```

The onDrawFrame() method can now call the draw method of Starfield and pass in the variable to scroll it. Notice that, because you are continuously adding values to the scroll variable, you must test it to make sure you have not maxed out the float and created an overrun:

```
@Override
public void onDrawFrame(GL10 unused) {
    float[] matrix = new float[16];

    GLES20.glClear(GLES20.GL_COLOR_BUFFER_BIT | GLES20.GL_DEPTH_BUFFER_BIT);

    Matrix.setLookAtM(mViewMatrix, 0, 0, 0, -3, 0f, 0f, 0f, 0f, 1.0f, 0.0f);

    Matrix.multiplyMM(mMVPMatrix, 0, mProjectionMatrix, 0, mViewMatrix, 0);

    starfield.draw(mMVPMatrix, starfieldScroll);
```

```
    if(starfieldScroll == Float.MAX_VALUE){
        starfieldScroll = 0;
    }

    starfieldScroll += .001;

}
```

The completed Starfield class and GameRenderer should appear as follows. If you have access to GitHub, you can also download it from https://github.com/jfdimarzio/AndroidStudioGameDev.

```java
public class GameRenderer implements GLSurfaceView.Renderer {

    private static final String TAG = "GameRenderer";
    private Context context;
    public static float[] mMVPMatrix = new float[16];
    public static float[] mProjectionMatrix = new float[16];
    public static float[] mViewMatrix = new float[16];

    private Starfield starfield;

    float starfieldScroll = 0;

    public GameRenderer(Context gameContext) {
        context = gameContext;
    }

    @Override
    public void onSurfaceCreated(GL10 unused, EGLConfig config) {
        GLES20.glClearColor(0.0f, 0.0f, 0.0f, 1.0f);

        starfield = new Starfield();

        starfield.loadTexture(R.drawable.starfield, context);
    }

    @Override
    public void onSurfaceChanged(GL10 unused, int width, int height) {
        GLES20.glViewport(0, 0, width, height);

        float ratio = (float) width / height;

        Matrix.frustumM(mProjectionMatrix, 0, -ratio, ratio, -1, 1, 3, 7);

    }
```

```
@Override
public void onDrawFrame(GL10 unused) {
    float[] matrix = new float[16];

    GLES20.glClear(GLES20.GL_COLOR_BUFFER_BIT | GLES20.GL_DEPTH_BUFFER_BIT);

    Matrix.setLookAtM(mViewMatrix, 0, 0, 0, -3, 0f, 0f, 0f, 0f, 1.0f, 0.0f);

    Matrix.multiplyMM(mMVPMatrix, 0, mProjectionMatrix, 0, mViewMatrix, 0);

    starfield.draw(mMVPMatrix, starfieldScroll);

    if(starfieldScroll == Float.MAX_VALUE){
        starfieldScroll = 0;
    }

    starfieldScroll += .001;

}

public static int loadShader(int type, String shaderCode){

    int shader = GLES20.glCreateShader(type);
    GLES20.glShaderSource(shader, shaderCode);
    GLES20.glCompileShader(shader);

    return shader;
}

public static void checkGlError(String glOperation) {
    int error;
    while ((error = GLES20.glGetError()) != GLES20.GL_NO_ERROR) {
        Log.e(TAG, glOperation + ": glError " + error);
        throw new RuntimeException(glOperation + ": glError " + error);
    }
}

}
```

This is the completed Starfield class:

```
public class Starfield {

    static float squareCoords[] = {
            -1f,  1f, 0.0f,   // top left
            -1f, -1f, 0.0f,   // bottom left
            1f, -1f, 0.0f,    // bottom right
            1f,  1f, 0.0f };  // top right

    private final short drawOrder[] = { 0, 1, 2, 0, 2, 3 };
```

```java
private final String vertexShaderCode =
        "uniform mat4 uMVPMatrix;" +
        "attribute vec4 vPosition;" +
        "attribute vec2 TexCoordIn;" +
        "varying vec2 TexCoordOut;" +
        "void main() {" +
        "  gl_Position = uMVPMatrix * vPosition;" +
        "  TexCoordOut = TexCoordIn;" +
        "}";

private final String fragmentShaderCode =
        "precision mediump float;" +
        "uniform vec4 vColor;" +
        "uniform sampler2D TexCoordIn;" +
        "uniform float scroll;" +
        "varying vec2 TexCoordOut;" +
        "void main() {" +
        " gl_FragColor = texture2D(TexCoordIn, " +
        "     vec2(TexCoordOut.x ,TexCoordOut.y + scroll));" +
        "}";
private float texture[] = {
        -1f, 1f,
        -1f, -1f,
        1f, -1f,
        1f, 1f,
};

private int[] textures = new int[1];
private final FloatBuffer vertexBuffer;
private final ShortBuffer drawListBuffer;
private final FloatBuffer textureBuffer;
private final int mProgram;
private int mPositionHandle;
private int mColorHandle;
private int mMVPMatrixHandle;

static final int COORDS_PER_TEXTURE = 2;
static final int COORDS_PER_VERTEX = 3;
private final int vertexStride = COORDS_PER_VERTEX * 4;
public static int textureStride = COORDS_PER_TEXTURE * 4;

public void loadTexture(int texture, Context context) {
    InputStream imagestream = context.getResources().openRawResource(texture);
    Bitmap bitmap = null;

    android.graphics.Matrix flip = new android.graphics.Matrix();
    flip.postScale(-1f, -1f);
```

```
    try {

        bitmap = BitmapFactory.decodeStream(imagestream);

    }catch(Exception e){

    }finally {
        try {
            imagestream.close();
            imagestream = null;
        } catch (IOException e) {
        }
    }

    GLES20.glGenTextures(1, textures, 0);
    GLES20.glBindTexture(GLES20.GL_TEXTURE_2D, textures[0]);

    GLES20.glTexParameterf(GLES20.GL_TEXTURE_2D,
            GLES20.GL_TEXTURE_MIN_FILTER, GLES20.GL_NEAREST);
    GLES20.glTexParameterf(GLES20.GL_TEXTURE_2D,
            GLES20.GL_TEXTURE_MAG_FILTER, GLES20.GL_LINEAR);

    GLES20.glTexParameterf(GLES20.GL_TEXTURE_2D,
            GLES20.GL_TEXTURE_WRAP_S, GLES20.GL_REPEAT);
    GLES20.glTexParameterf(GLES20.GL_TEXTURE_2D,
            GLES20.GL_TEXTURE_WRAP_T, GLES20.GL_REPEAT);

    GLUtils.texImage2D(GLES20.GL_TEXTURE_2D, 0, bitmap, 0);

    bitmap.recycle();
}
public Starfield() {
    ByteBuffer bb = ByteBuffer.allocateDirect(squareCoords.length * 4);
    bb.order(ByteOrder.nativeOrder());
    vertexBuffer = bb.asFloatBuffer();
    vertexBuffer.put(squareCoords);
    vertexBuffer.position(0);

    bb = ByteBuffer.allocateDirect(texture.length * 4);
    bb.order(ByteOrder.nativeOrder());
    textureBuffer = bb.asFloatBuffer();
    textureBuffer.put(texture);
    textureBuffer.position(0);

    ByteBuffer dlb = ByteBuffer.allocateDirect(drawOrder.length * 2);
    dlb.order(ByteOrder.nativeOrder());
    drawListBuffer = dlb.asShortBuffer();
    drawListBuffer.put(drawOrder);
    drawListBuffer.position(0);
```

```java
    int vertexShader = GameRenderer.loadShader(GLES20.GL_VERTEX_SHADER,
                        vertexShaderCode);
    int fragmentShader = GameRenderer.loadShader(GLES20.GL_FRAGMENT_
                        SHADER, fragmentShaderCode);

    mProgram = GLES20.glCreateProgram();
    GLES20.glAttachShader(mProgram, vertexShader);
    GLES20.glAttachShader(mProgram, fragmentShader);
    GLES20.glLinkProgram(mProgram);
}

public void draw(float[] mvpMatrix, float scroll) {

    GLES20.glUseProgram(mProgram);

    mPositionHandle = GLES20.glGetAttribLocation(mProgram, "vPosition");

    GLES20.glEnableVertexAttribArray(mPositionHandle);

    int vsTextureCoord = GLES20.glGetAttribLocation(mProgram,
                        "TexCoordIn");

    GLES20.glVertexAttribPointer(mPositionHandle, COORDS_PER_VERTEX,
            GLES20.GL_FLOAT, false,
            vertexStride, vertexBuffer);

    GLES20.glVertexAttribPointer(vsTextureCoord, COORDS_PER_TEXTURE,
            GLES20.GL_FLOAT, false,
            textureStride, textureBuffer);

    GLES20.glEnableVertexAttribArray(vsTextureCoord);

    GLES20.glActiveTexture(GLES20.GL_TEXTURE0);
    GLES20.glBindTexture(GLES20.GL_TEXTURE_2D, textures[0]);
    int fsTexture = GLES20.glGetUniformLocation(mProgram, "TexCoordOut");
    int fsScroll = GLES20.glGetUniformLocation(mProgram, "scroll");
    GLES20.glUniform1i(fsTexture, 0);
    GLES20.glUniform1f(fsScroll, scroll);
    mMVPMatrixHandle = GLES20.glGetUniformLocation(mProgram, "uMVPMatrix");
    GameRenderer.checkGlError("glGetUniformLocation");
    GLES20.glUniformMatrix4fv(mMVPMatrixHandle, 1, false, mvpMatrix, 0);
    GameRenderer.checkGlError("glUniformMatrix4fv");
    GLES20.glDrawElements(GLES20.GL_TRIANGLES, drawOrder.length, GLES20.
    GL_UNSIGNED_SHORT, drawListBuffer);

    GLES20.glDisableVertexAttribArray(mPositionHandle);
}

}
```

Working with Spritesheets

A *spritesheet* is a specialized image that contains multiple images within one bitmap. Figure 7-3 illustrates a spritesheet.

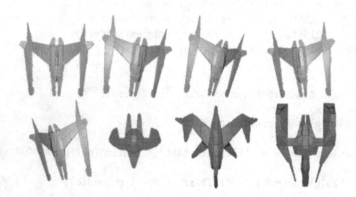

Figure 7-3. A character spritesheet

The advantage of using a spritesheet is that you can zoom in to focus on only one of the images, and then change the look of a character by scrolling to another image in the sheet.

Here is another class, named Hero, based on the Starfield class which uses a spritesheet to display a spaceship. Add this class to your game. The only differences between this class and Starfield are the size of the texture and the way the texture is moved to display the correct image.

The bitmap in Figure 7-3 shows a spritesheet that has the potential to display 4×4 images. This means the location of the upper-left corner of each image can be plotted on a matrix by using x, y coordinates as follows: (0,0) for the first image in the first row, (0,25) for the second image in the first row, (25,0) for the first image in the second row, and so on.

In the onDrawFrame() method, you will use these coordinates in the matrix multiplication to display the correct image:

```
public class Hero {

    static float squareCoords[] = {
            -0.25f,  0.25f, 0.0f,   // top left
            -0.25f, -0.25f, 0.0f,   // bottom left
            0.25f, -0.25f, 0.0f,    // bottom right
            0.25f,  0.25f, 0.0f };  // top right
```

```java
private final short drawOrder[] = { 0, 1, 2, 0, 2, 3 };

private final String vertexShaderCode =
        "uniform mat4 uMVPMatrix;" +
                "attribute vec4 vPosition;" +
                "attribute vec2 TexCoordIn;" +
                "varying vec2 TexCoordOut;" +
                "void main() {" +
                "   gl_Position = uMVPMatrix * vPosition;" +
                "   TexCoordOut = TexCoordIn;" +
                "}";

private final String fragmentShaderCode =
        "precision mediump float;" +
                "uniform vec4 vColor;" +
                "uniform sampler2D TexCoordIn;" +
                "uniform float posX;" +
                "uniform float posY;" +
                "varying vec2 TexCoordOut;" +
                "void main() {" +
                "   gl_FragColor = texture2D(TexCoordIn,
                    vec2(TexCoordOut.x + posX ,TexCoordOut.y + posY ));" +
                "}";
private float texture[] = {
        0f, 0.25f,
        0f, 0f,
        0.25f, 0f,
        0.25f, 0.25f,
};

private int[] textures = new int[1];
private final FloatBuffer vertexBuffer;
private final ShortBuffer drawListBuffer;
private final FloatBuffer textureBuffer;
private final int mProgram;
private int mPositionHandle;
private int mMVPMatrixHandle;

static final int COORDS_PER_TEXTURE = 2;
static final int COORDS_PER_VERTEX = 3;
private final int vertexStride = COORDS_PER_VERTEX * 4;
public static int textureStride = COORDS_PER_TEXTURE * 4;

public void loadTexture(int texture, Context context) {
    InputStream imagestream = context.getResources().
    openRawResource(texture);
    Bitmap bitmap = null;
```

```java
        android.graphics.Matrix flip = new android.graphics.Matrix();
        flip.postScale(-1f, -1f);

        try {

            bitmap = BitmapFactory.decodeStream(imagestream);

        }catch(Exception e){

        }finally {
            try {
                imagestream.close();
                imagestream = null;
            } catch (IOException e) {
            }
        }

        GLES20.glGenTextures(1, textures, 0);
        GLES20.glBindTexture(GLES20.GL_TEXTURE_2D, textures[0]);

        GLES20.glTexParameterf(GLES20.GL_TEXTURE_2D, GLES20.GL_TEXTURE_MIN_
        FILTER, GLES20.GL_LINEAR);
        GLES20.glTexParameterf(GLES20.GL_TEXTURE_2D, GLES20.GL_TEXTURE_MAG_
        FILTER, GLES20.GL_LINEAR);

        GLES20.glTexParameterf(GLES20.GL_TEXTURE_2D, GLES20.GL_TEXTURE_
        WRAP_S, GLES20.GL_CLAMP_TO_EDGE);
        GLES20.glTexParameterf(GLES20.GL_TEXTURE_2D, GLES20.GL_TEXTURE_
        WRAP_T, GLES20.GL_CLAMP_TO_EDGE);

        GLUtils.texImage2D(GLES20.GL_TEXTURE_2D, 0, bitmap, 0);

        bitmap.recycle();
    }
    public Hero() {
        ByteBuffer bb = ByteBuffer.allocateDirect(squareCoords.length * 4);
        bb.order(ByteOrder.nativeOrder());
        vertexBuffer = bb.asFloatBuffer();
        vertexBuffer.put(squareCoords);
        vertexBuffer.position(0);

        bb = ByteBuffer.allocateDirect(texture.length * 4);
        bb.order(ByteOrder.nativeOrder());
        textureBuffer = bb.asFloatBuffer();
        textureBuffer.put(texture);
        textureBuffer.position(0);
```

```
        ByteBuffer dlb = ByteBuffer.allocateDirect(drawOrder.length * 2);
        dlb.order(ByteOrder.nativeOrder());
        drawListBuffer = dlb.asShortBuffer();
        drawListBuffer.put(drawOrder);
        drawListBuffer.position(0);

        int vertexShader = GameRenderer.loadShader(GLES20.GL_VERTEX_SHADER,
        vertexShaderCode);
        int fragmentShader = GameRenderer.loadShader(GLES20.GL_FRAGMENT_
        SHADER, fragmentShaderCode);

        mProgram = GLES20.glCreateProgram();
        GLES20.glAttachShader(mProgram, vertexShader);
        GLES20.glAttachShader(mProgram, fragmentShader);
        GLES20.glLinkProgram(mProgram);
    }

    public void draw(float[] mvpMatrix, float posX, float posY) {

        GLES20.glUseProgram(mProgram);

        mPositionHandle = GLES20.glGetAttribLocation(mProgram, "vPosition");

        GLES20.glEnableVertexAttribArray(mPositionHandle);

        int vsTextureCoord = GLES20.glGetAttribLocation(mProgram, "TexCoordIn");

        GLES20.glVertexAttribPointer(mPositionHandle, COORDS_PER_VERTEX,
                GLES20.GL_FLOAT, false,
                vertexStride, vertexBuffer);

        GLES20.glVertexAttribPointer(vsTextureCoord, COORDS_PER_TEXTURE,
                GLES20.GL_FLOAT, false,
                textureStride, textureBuffer);

        GLES20.glEnableVertexAttribArray(vsTextureCoord);

        GLES20.glActiveTexture(GLES20.GL_TEXTURE0);

        int fsTexture = GLES20.glGetUniformLocation(mProgram, "TexCoordOut");
        int fsPosX = GLES20.glGetUniformLocation(mProgram, "posX");
        int fsPosY = GLES20.glGetUniformLocation(mProgram, "posY");
        GLES20.glUniform1i(fsTexture, 0);
        GLES20.glUniform1f(fsPosX, posX);
        GLES20.glUniform1f(fsPosY, posY);
        mMVPMatrixHandle = GLES20.glGetUniformLocation(mProgram, "uMVPMatrix");
        GameRenderer.checkGlError("glGetUniformLocation");
        GLES20.glUniformMatrix4fv(mMVPMatrixHandle, 1, false, mvpMatrix, 0);
        GameRenderer.checkGlError("glUniformMatrix4fv");
```

```
        GLES20.glBindTexture(GLES20.GL_TEXTURE_2D, textures[0]);

        GLES20.glDrawElements(GLES20.GL_TRIANGLES,
                drawOrder.length, GLES20.GL_UNSIGNED_SHORT, drawListBuffer);

        GLES20.glDisableVertexAttribArray(mPositionHandle);
    }
}
```

Change the GameRenderer to look like this:

```
public class GameRenderer implements GLSurfaceView.Renderer {

    private static final String TAG = "GameRenderer";
    private Context context;
    public static float[] mMVPMatrix = new float[16];
    public static float[] mProjectionMatrix = new float[16];
    public static float[] mViewMatrix = new float[16];
    public static float[] mTranslationMatrix = new float[16];

    private Starfield starfield;
    private Hero hero;

    float starfieldScroll = 0;

    float heroSprite = 0;

    public GameRenderer(Context gameContext) {
        context = gameContext;

    }

    @Override
    public void onSurfaceCreated(GL10 unused, EGLConfig config) {
        GLES20.glClearColor(0.0f, 0.0f, 0.0f, 1.0f);

        starfield = new Starfield();
        hero = new Hero();

        starfield.loadTexture(R.drawable.starfield, context);
        hero.loadTexture(R.drawable.ships, context);
    }
    @Override
    public void onSurfaceChanged(GL10 unused, int width, int height) {
        GLES20.glViewport(0, 0, width, height);
```

```java
    float ratio = (float) width / height;

    Matrix.frustumM(mProjectionMatrix, 0, -ratio, ratio, -1, 1, 3, 7);

}

@Override
public void onDrawFrame(GL10 unused) {
    float[] matrix = new float[16];

    GLES20.glClear(GLES20.GL_COLOR_BUFFER_BIT | GLES20.GL_DEPTH_BUFFER_BIT);

    Matrix.setLookAtM(mViewMatrix, 0, 0, 0, -3, 0f, 0f, 0f, 0f, 1.0f, 0.0f);

    Matrix.multiplyMM(mMVPMatrix, 0, mProjectionMatrix, 0, mViewMatrix, 0);

    starfield.draw(mMVPMatrix, starfieldScroll);

    GLES20.glEnable(GLES20.GL_BLEND);
    GLES20.glBlendFunc(GLES20.GL_SRC_ALPHA, GLES20.GL_ONE_MINUS_SRC_ALPHA);
    Matrix.setIdentityM(mTranslationMatrix,0);
    Matrix.translateM(mTranslationMatrix, 0,0,-.5f,0);

    Matrix.multiplyMM(matrix, 0, mMVPMatrix, 0, mTranslationMatrix, 0);

    hero.draw(matrix,0,0);

    GLES20.glDisable(GLES20.GL_BLEND);

    if(starfieldScroll == Float.MAX_VALUE){
        starfieldScroll = 0;
    }

    starfieldScroll += .001;

}

public static int loadShader(int type, String shaderCode){

    int shader = GLES20.glCreateShader(type);

    // add the source code to the shader and compile it
    GLES20.glShaderSource(shader, shaderCode);
    GLES20.glCompileShader(shader);

    return shader;
}
```

```
public static void checkGlError(String glOperation) {
    int error;
    while ((error = GLES20.glGetError()) != GLES20.GL_NO_ERROR) {
        Log.e(TAG, glOperation + ": glError " + error);
        throw new RuntimeException(glOperation + ": glError " + error);
    }
}

}
```

One final thing to note: the line GLES20.glBlendFunc(GLES20.GL_SRC_ALPHA, GLES20.GL_ONE_MINUS_SRC_ALPHA) in the onDrawFrame() method helps with the transparency. The spritesheet has a transparent background to allow the star field to be seen through it. If you did not use the blend function, the background of the spritesheet would render as black in this case.

In the next chapter, you are going to test for player input.

Chapter 8

Reading User Input

If you have never coded a game for a mobile device or tablet, one problem will quickly arise. Unlike for gaming consoles, or even desktops, a distinct lack of input options exist to relay your player's intentions back into the game code. Without the benefit of game controllers, keyboards, or mice, supplying your player with a complex input system can be difficult.

The majority of your player input will come from the device's touch screen. Wiring up your game to detect and respond to touch events on the device is not as hard as it may appear on the surface.

Using the onTouchEvent()

Within your GameView class, override the onTouchEvent() as follows:

```
@Override
public boolean onTouchEvent(MotionEvent event) {
}
```

The onTouchEvent() takes in a MotionEvent. This MotionEvent is automatically passed in by the system when the event call is generated.

The MotionEvent contains all the information that you need to help determine and decipher the action of the player. From the MotionEvent, you get information such as the x and y coordinates where the player touched, and the pressure and duration of that touch. You can even determine the direction of a swipe movement.

In this example, you are just going to get the player's touch coordinates:

```
@Override
public boolean onTouchEvent(MotionEvent event) {

            float x = event.getX();
            float y = event.getY();
}
```

You can now react to the x and y coordinates as you see fit.

If you want to detect multiple touch points, use getPointerCount() and PointerCoords to help retrieve the pointer objects for detecting multitouch input.

The MotionEvent that is passed into onTouchEvent() can track up to five distinct simultaneous screen touches. The concept here is to loop through all of the pointers that were detected using getPointerCount(). Inside the loop you are going to use getPointerID() to retrieve the information that you need for each pointer.

Begin by setting up your onTouchEvent() and looping through the detected pointers:

```
@Override
public boolean onTouchEvent(MotionEvent event) {

    MotionEvent.PointerCoords[] coords = new
            MotionEvent.PointerCoords[event.getPointerCount()];

    For(int i = 0; i< event.getPointerCount(); i++)
    {
        event.getPointerCoords(i, coords[i]);
    }
}
```

You can now get all of the information that you need, from each pointer that was detected.

Let's say you are creating a platform game in which the player can run to the left and to the right. You have set up your onTouchEvent() and you are trapping the x and y coordinates each time the player touches the screen. How can you easily determine whether those coordinates should push the player to the left or to the right?

The answer is to divide the screen into *touch zones*—in this case, one zone on the left side of the screen and one zone on the right. A couple of simple if statements can then be used to check the locations on the screen that the player touched.

Using the example of a platform game, in which the only directions the player can move are to the left and to the right, you can divide the screen into two halves—one representing the left and one the right. You may also want to consider placing the touch zones toward the bottom of the screen, where a player's thumbs may be.

This means that you would have to ignore any touch coordinates that fall above the left and right touch zones. Take a look at Figures 8-1 and 8-2 for a visual representation of this concept.

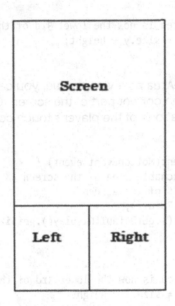

Figure 8-1. Portrait mode left and right touch zones

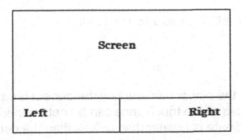

Figure 8-2. Landscape mode left and right touch zones

The first step is to get the height of the screen:

```
@Override
public boolean onTouchEvent(MotionEvent event) {
        //get the non-touchable area of the screen -
        //the upper 2/3rds of the screen
        Point size = new Point();
activity.getWindowManager().getDefaultDisplay().getSize(size);
int width = size.x;
int height = size.y / 3;

        //the playable area is now the lower 3rd of the screen
        int playableArea = size.y - height;
}
```

Using the value playableArea as a y axis value, you can easily tell whether your player is touching the correct part of the screen. Create a simple if statement to test the locations of the player's touch coordinates:

```
 @Override
public boolean onTouchEvent(MotionEvent event) {
        //get the non-touchable area of the screen -
        //the upper 2/3rds of the screen
        Point size = new Point();
activity.getWindowManager().getDefaultDisplay().getSize(size);
int width = size.x;
int height = size.y / 3;

        //the playable area is now the lower 3rd of the screen
        int playableArea = size.y - height;

        if (y > playableArea){

        //this y coordiate is within the touch zone

        }
}
```

Now that you know the player has touched the correct area of the screen, the left and right sides of the touch zone can be determined by testing whether the x coordinate is greater than or less than the center point of the screen:

```
@Override
public boolean onTouchEvent(MotionEvent event) {
        //get the non-touchable area of the screen -
        //the upper 2/3rds of the screen
```

```
Point size = new Point();
activity.getWindowManager().getDefaultDisplay().getSize(size);

//get the center point of the screen
int width = size.x / 2;

int height = size.y / 3;

//the playable area is now the lower 3rd of the screen
int playableArea = size.y - height;

if (y > playableArea){

//this y coordinate is within the touch zone

    if(x < center){
        //The player touched the left
    }else{
        //The player touched the right
    }

}
}
```

You have successfully determined whether the player has touched the left or right side of the screen. Replace the comments with your specific code to initiate actions based on where the player touched.

For some games (think Temple Run) you want to let players swipe or fling the screen to indicate which direction they want to move. A fling upward could represent a jump, for example. This could be a much more versatile method of player input, but it also requires a bit more setup code.

Adding a Gesture Listener

Open your GameView and instantiate a SimpleInGestureListener:

```
GestureDetector.SimpleOnGestureListener gestureListener = new
            GestureDetector.SimpleOnGestureListener(){

};
```

There are several methods that you need to implement within the gesture listener. However, the only one you will be working with in this solution is OnFling():

```
GestureDetector.SimpleOnGestureListener gestureListener = new
            GestureDetector.SimpleOnGestureListener(){
    @Override
    public boolean onDown(MotionEvent arg0) {
            // TODO Auto-generated method stub
            return false;
    }

    @Override
    public boolean onFling(MotionEvent e1, MotionEvent e2, float velocityX,
                float velocityY) {
            //React to the fling action
            return false;
    }
    @Override
    public void onLongPress(MotionEvent e) {
            // TODO Auto-generated method stub

    }
    @Override
    public boolean onScroll(MotionEvent e1, MotionEvent e2, float distanceX,
                float distanceY) {
            // TODO Auto-generated method stub
            return false;
    }
    @Override
    public void onShowPress(MotionEvent e) {
            // TODO Auto-generated method stub

    }
    @Override
    public boolean onSingleTapUp(MotionEvent e) {
            // TODO Auto-generated method stub
            return false;
    }
};
```

Now, create a new variable:

```
private GestureDetector gd;
```

The GestureDetector will be used to throw the gesture event. Initialize the detector in the onCreate() of the activity:

```
@Override
public void onCreate(Bundle savedInstanceState) {
    super.onCreate(savedInstanceState);
    gd = new GestureDetector(this,gestureListener);
}
```

Finally, in the OnTouchEvent(), throw to the gestureListener:

```
@Override
public boolean onTouchEvent(MotionEvent event) {
    return gd.onTouchEvent(event);
}
```

When the player flings the screen, the code in OnFling() will be executed. This takes care of the "what" and "when." Now you need to determine which direction.

Notice that OnFling() takes two MotionEvent attributes. Because you have used it earlier, you know that the MotionEvent contains a getX() and a getY() for getting you the respective coordinates of the event.

The two events—e1 and e2—represent the starting point and ending point of the fling. Therefore, using the x and y coordinates of each event, you can calculate which direction the player moved.

```
float leftMotion = e1.getX() - e2.getX();
    float upMotion = e1.getY() - e2.getY();

    float rightMotion = e2.getX() - e1.getX();
    float downMotion = e2.getY() - e1.getY();

    if((leftMotion == Math.max(leftMotion, rightMotion)) &&
       (leftMotion > Math.max(downMotion, upMotion)) )
    {
        //The player moved left
    }

    if((rightMotion == Math.max(leftMotion, rightMotion))
        && rightMotion > Math.max(downMotion, upMotion) )
{
        //The player moved right
}
```

```
if((upMotion == Math.max(upMotion, downMotion))
    && (upMotion > Math.max(leftMotion, rightMotion)) )
{
        //The player moved up
}

if((downMotion == Math.max(upMotion, downMotion))
    && (downMotion > Math.max(leftMotion, rightMotion)) )
{
        //The player moved down
}
```

Now you can fill in the appropriate code for the action you need to take in your game.

In the next chapter, you will move the image on the screen based on the touch even being detected.

Chapter 9

In-Game Movement

In the preceding chapter, you looked at several methods for detecting whether a player has interacted with the screen. In this chapter, you will have your character react to that movement. Let's look at the Hero class from Chapter 7 again.

The Hero class is a spaceship that a player can move around the screen. Moving the image on the screen is going to be easier than it sounds. All you need to do is increment (or decrement) a single value in the transformation matrix when the Hero is drawn. You are updating only one value in this case, because you are going to be moving the ship on only one axis. If you were moving the ship on two axes, you would need to update two values in the matrix.

Let's start by adding a getter and setter to the GameRenderer class for a float named heroMove. This float tracks how much the ship should be moved:

```
float heroMove = 0;
public void setHeroMove(float movement){
    heroMove = movement;
}
public float getHeroMove(){
    return heroMove;
}
```

Now, update the heroMove float by using the getter and setter from the onTouchEvent() in the game view. I have chosen to go with a simple onTouchEvent() for this example. It detects only that the player touched the left or right side of the screen:

```
public boolean onTouchEvent(MotionEvent e) {

        float x = e.getX();
        switch (e.getAction()) {
            case MotionEvent.ACTION_DOWN:

                if (x < getWidth() / 2) {
                  gameRenderer.setHeroMove(gameRenderer.getHeroMove() + .1f);
                }

                if (x > getWidth() /2){
                gameRenderer.setHeroMove(gameRenderer.getHeroMove() - .1f);

                }
        }

        return true;
    }
}
```

The heroMove float is now updated each time the player touches the screen. Let's use this to update the position of the Hero by modifying the transformation matrix in the GameRenderer:

```
public void onDrawFrame(GL10 unused) {
    float[] matrix = new float[16];

    GLES20.glClear(GLES20.GL_COLOR_BUFFER_BIT | GLES20.GL_DEPTH_BUFFER_BIT);

    Matrix.setLookAtM(mViewMatrix, 0, 0, 0, -3, 0f, 0f, 0f, 0f, 1.0f, 0.0f);

    Matrix.multiplyMM(mMVPMatrix, 0, mProjectionMatrix, 0, mViewMatrix, 0);

    starfield.draw(mMVPMatrix, starfieldScroll);

    GLES20.glEnable(GLES20.GL_BLEND);
    GLES20.glBlendFunc(GLES20.GL_SRC_ALPHA, GLES20.GL_ONE_MINUS_SRC_ALPHA);

    //debris.draw(mMVPMatrix, debrisScroll);
    Matrix.setIdentityM(mTranslationMatrix,0);
    Matrix.translateM(mTranslationMatrix, 0,heroMove,-.5f,0);
```

```
Matrix.multiplyMM(matrix, 0, mMVPMatrix, 0, mTranslationMatrix, 0);

hero.draw(matrix,0,0);

GLES20.glDisable(GLES20.GL_BLEND);

if(starfieldScroll == Float.MAX_VALUE){
    starfieldScroll = 0;
}
if(debrisScroll == Float.MAX_VALUE){
    debrisScroll = 0;
}
starfieldScroll += .001;
debrisScroll += .01;

}
```

The float heroMove is multiplied into the translation matrix to move the image on the x axis. There is a hard-coded value of -.5f in the y axis in this example to keep the ship at the bottom of the screen. However, if you wanted to move the ship on the y axis as well, you would simply create another float and put it in place of the -.5f.

In the final chapter of this mini-book, you will look at some solutions for collision detection.

Chapter 10

Collision Detection

Collision detection is a key component to almost any game and almost every game type. In a game without collision detection, items, obstacles, characters, and weapons would move about the screen and float past each other without any consequence.

Your game code needs to be able to determine whether objects that are on the screen touch or cross paths with each other. It is only after you determine that two or more objects are touching that you can then perform actions on them such as applying damage, stopping motion, powering up a character, or destroying an object.

Using Basic Collision Detection

Basic collision detection is useful if you are creating a game in which a character is faced with static obstacles such as floors and platforms, the edges of the screen, or steps. You can use constant values when you are testing for the location of static objects. For example, you can use basic collision detection to determine when the character has finished jumping and is back on the ground. This code would be placed in either a separate jump method, or in the onTouchEvent():

```
previousJumpPos = posJump;

posJump += (float)(((Math.PI / 2) / .5) * PLAYER_RUN_SPEED);
if (posJump <= Math.PI)
    {
            goodguy. posY += 1.5 / .5 * .15 * PLAYER_RUN_SPEED;
```

```
        }else{
                goodguy. posY -=(Math.sin((double)posJump) -
                Math.sin((double)previousJumpPos))* 1.5;
                if (goodguy.y <= .75f){
                        playeraction = PLAYER_STAND;
                        goodguy. posY = .75f;
                }
        }
        goodguy. posX += PLAYER_RUN_SPEED;
        Matrix.translateM(RotationMatrix, 0, goodguy. posX, goodguy. posY, 0);
```

What about running off the edge of the screen? If the action of your game needs to be contained to a single screen, and the x axis in OpenGL ES has been scaled to range from 0 (far left) to 4 (far right), you can test your character against that to stop the image from leaving the screen.

```
if(goodguy.posX <= 0 )
{
//the player has reached the left edge of the screen
//correct the image's position and perform whatever action is necessary

goodguy. posX = 0;
}
```

This process requires an extra step if you are testing for a collision against the right edge of the screen. The x position of the character in OpenGL ES represents the lower-left corner of the image. Therefore, if you are testing whether the image of the character has encountered the right-hand side of the screen, the x position of the character, at the lower-left side, will not reach the right edge of the screen until the entire image has already passed off the screen.

You can compensate for this by adding the size of the character image to the `if` statement that tests for the collision:

```
if(goodguy. posX +.25f >= 4 )
{
//the player has reached the right edge of the screen
//correct the image's position and perform whatever action is necessary

goodguy. posX = (4f - .25f);
}
```

The basic method of collision detection is effective for less-complex game logic, where there many static objects, the size and location of which are easily known to the game loop.

What if your game logic is not that easy, and you are dealing with multiple moving items?

Using More Robust Collision Detection

To implement a more robust form of collision detection, create a new method that can be called from your game loop. The method will loop through all of the active items on the screen and determine whether any are colliding.

The key fields needed to implement this kind of collision detection are the x and y axis coordinates of the objects' current locations, and the status of the objects. The status refers to whether or not the object is eligible to be included in collision detection. This could include a flag that the object has already been destroyed or perhaps the character being tested has a power up that allows them to be free of collision detection for a specific period of time.

The following code depicts a version of the Hero class, called Enemy. Three public values have been added to the class: one each for the x and y axis coordinates to track the character's current position, and a Boolean to indicate whether the character has been destroyed.

```
public class Enemy {

    public float posY = 0;
    public float posX = 0;
    public bool isDestroyed = false;

    private final String vertexShaderCode =
            "uniform mat4 uMVPMatrix;" +
            "attribute vec4 vPosition;" +
            "attribute vec2 TexCoordIn;" +
            "varying vec2 TexCoordOut;" +
            "void main() {" +
            "  gl_Position = uMVPMatrix * vPosition;" +
            "  TexCoordOut = TexCoordIn;" +
            "}";

    private final String fragmentShaderCode =
            "precision mediump float;" +
            "uniform vec4 vColor;" +
            "uniform sampler2D TexCoordIn;" +
            "varying vec2 TexCoordOut;" +
            "void main() {" +
            "  gl_FragColor = texture2D(TexCoordIn, TexCoordOut);" +
            "}";

    private float texture[] = {
            0, 0,
            1f, 0,
            1f, 1f,
            0, 1f,
                        };
```

```java
private int[] textures = new int[1];
private final FloatBuffer vertexBuffer;
private final ShortBuffer drawListBuffer;
private final FloatBuffer textureBuffer;
private final int program;
private int positionHandle;
private int matrixHandle;

static final int COORDS_PER_VERTEX = 3;
static final int COORDS_PER_TEXTURE = 2;
static float vertices[] = { -1f,  1f, 0.0,
                            -1f, -1f, 0.0,
                             1f, -1f, 0.0,
                             1f,  1f, 0.0 };

private final short indices[] = { 0, 1, 2, 0, 2, 3 };

private final int vertexStride = COORDS_PER_VERTEX * 4;
public static int textureStride = COORDS_PER_TEXTURE * 4;

public void loadTexture(int texture, Context context) {
        InputStream imagestream = context.getResources().
        openRawResource(texture);
        Bitmap bitmap = null;

        android.graphics.Matrix flip = new android.graphics.Matrix();
        flip.postScale(-1f, -1f);

        try {

            bitmap = BitmapFactory.decodeStream(imagestream);

        }catch(Exception e){

        }finally {
          try {
                imagestream.close();
                imagestream = null;
          } catch (IOException e) {
          }
        }

        GLES20.glGenTextures(1, textures, 0);
        GLES20.glBindTexture(GLES20.GL_TEXTURE_2D, textures[0]);

        GLES20.glTexParameterf(GLES20.GL_TEXTURE_2D,
              GLES20.GL_TEXTURE_MIN_FILTER, GLES20.GL_NEAREST);
        GLES20.glTexParameterf(GLES20.GL_TEXTURE_2D,
              GLES20.GL_TEXTURE_MAG_FILTER, GLES20.GL_LINEAR);
```

```java
            GLES20.glTexParameterf(GLES20.GL_TEXTURE_2D,
                    GLES20.GL_TEXTURE_WRAP_S, GLES20.GL_REPEAT);
            GLES20.glTexParameterf(GLES20.GL_TEXTURE_2D,
                    GLES20.GL_TEXTURE_WRAP_T, GLES20.GL_REPEAT);

            GLUtils.texImage2D(GLES20.GL_TEXTURE_2D, 0, bitmap, 0);

            bitmap.recycle();
        }

public Enemy () {

        ByteBuffer byteBuff = ByteBuffer.allocateDirect(
        byteBuff.order(ByteOrder.nativeOrder());
        vertexBuffer = byteBuff.asFloatBuffer();
        vertexBuffer.put(vertices);
        vertexBuffer.position(0);

        byteBuff = ByteBuffer.allocateDirect(texture.length * 4);
        byteBuff.order(ByteOrder.nativeOrder());
            textureBuffer = byteBuff.asFloatBuffer();
            textureBuffer.put(texture);
            textureBuffer.position(0);

        ByteBuffer indexBuffer = ByteBuffer.allocateDirect(
        indexBuffer.order(ByteOrder.nativeOrder());
        drawListBuffer = indexBuffer.asShortBuffer();
        drawListBuffer.put(indices);
        drawListBuffer.position(0);

        int vertexShader = SBGGameRenderer.loadShader(GLES20.GL_VERTEX_SHADER,
                                                vertexShaderCode);
        int fragmentShader = SBGGameRenderer.loadShader(GLES20.GL_FRAGMENT_SHADER,
                                                fragmentShaderCode);

        program = GLES20.glCreateProgram();
        GLES20.glAttachShader(program, vertexShader);
        GLES20.glAttachShader(program, fragmentShader);
        GLES20.glLinkProgram(program);
    }

    public void draw(float[] matrix) {

        GLES20.glUseProgram(program);

        positionHandle = GLES20.glGetAttribLocation(program, "vPosition");

        GLES20.glEnableVertexAttribArray(positionHandle);
```

```
    int vsTextureCoord = GLES20.glGetAttribLocation(program, "TexCoordIn");

    GLES20.glVertexAttribPointer(positionHandle, COORDS_PER_VERTEX,
                            GLES20.GL_FLOAT, false,
                            vertexStride, vertexBuffer);
    GLES20.glVertexAttribPointer(vsTextureCoord, COORDS_PER_TEXTURE,
            GLES20.GL_FLOAT, false,
            textureStride, textureBuffer);
    GLES20.glEnableVertexAttribArray(vsTextureCoord);
    GLES20.glActiveTexture(GLES20.GL_TEXTURE0);
    GLES20.glBindTexture(GLES20.GL_TEXTURE_2D, textures[0]);
    int fsTexture = GLES20.glGetUniformLocation(program, "TexCoordOut");
            GLES20.glUniform1i(fsTexture, 0);

    matrixHandle = GLES20.glGetUniformLocation(program, "uMVPMatrix");

    GLES20.glUniformMatrix4fv(matrixHandle, 1, false, matrix, 0);

    GLES20.glDrawElements(GLES20.GL_TRIANGLES, drawOrder.length,
                        GLES20.GL_UNSIGNED_SHORT, drawListBuffer);

    GLES20.glDisableVertexAttribArray(positionHandle);
    }
}
```

Now, build a new class that can be called from the game loop to see if this Enemy has run into another object, like a missile fired by the Hero. The easiest way to accomplish the collision test is to create—in memory—a bounding box around each active object and then test whether the edge of any two objects' bounding box collide. Why bounding boxes? It is easier to test straight lines, such as boxes, than to calculate the true edges of complex shapes. Also, objects in the game will typically collide so quickly that the eye will not be able to detect that the collision occurred a fraction of a millimeter away from the visible border of the actual object.

Create the bounding box by adding the size (in coordinates) to the current x and y coordinate position of the object. This means that an object that is scaled to 0.25 square on the coordinate axis will have a bounding box from x to (x + 0.25) and from y to (y + 0.25). Anything that crosses into that space will collide with that object. To test for a collision in this example, all you need to do is check whether another object's bounding box contains a point that is between (x to (x + 0.25)) and (y to (y + 0.25)). If so, those two objects collided.

In the following code sample, the shot being fired has a 0.25 coordinate value bounding box, and the enemy has a 1 coordinate value bounding box.

The following code assumes that the Hero can have fired up to four shots onscreen at one time, meaning that there are potentially four objects that the Enemy can be hit by:

```
private void detectCollisions(){
    for (int y = 1; y < 4; y ++){ //loop through the 4 potential shots in
    the array
        if (playerFire[y].shotFired){ //only test the shots that are
        currently active
            if(!enemy.isDestroyed){ //only test the shot against the enemy
            if it is not already destroyed
                //test for the collision
                if (((playerFire[y].posY  >= enemy.posY
                    && playerFire[y].posY <= enemy.posY + 1f )  ||
                    (playerFire[y].posY +.25f  >= enemy.posY
                    && playerFire[y].posY + .25f <= enemy.posY + 1f )) &&
                    ((playerFire[y].posX >= enemy.posX
                    && playerFire[y].posX <= enemy.posX + 1f) ||
                    (playerFire[y].posX + .25f >= enemy.posX
                    && playerFire[y].posX + 25f <= enemy.posX + 1f ))){

                    //collision detected between enemy and a shot

                }
            }
        }
    }
}
```

This method works well when detecting a collision between a round of shots and a single enemy. To test for a collision between a round of shots and numerous enemies, you will need to modify the method slightly to loop through your array of enemies:

```
private void detectCollisions(){
    for (int y = 1; y < 4; y ++){
        if (playerFire[y].shotFired){
            //assumes you have an array of 10 enemies
            for (int x = 1; x < 10; x++ ){
                if(!enemies[x].isDestroyed){
                    if (((playerFire[y].posY  >= enemies[x].posY &&
                    playerFire[y].posY <= enemies[x].posY + 1f )  ||
                    (playerFire[y].posY +.25f  >= enemies[x].posY &&
                    playerFire[y].posY + .25f <= enemies[x].posY + 1f )) &&
                    ((playerFire[y].posX >= enemies[x].posX &&
```

```
            playerFire[y].posX <= enemies[x].posX + 1f) ||
            (playerFire[y].posX + .25f >= enemies[x].posX  &&
            playerFire[y].posX + 25f <= enemies[x].posX + 1f ))){

            //collision detected between enemy and a shot

            }
        }
      }
    }
  }
}
```

This collision detection method will help you test for collisions between the bounding boxes of multiple objects in your game.

I hope you have found the concepts in this mini-book useful. Although we have not been able to cover the complete game development process from beginning to bed, a great deal of information has been crammed into these pages. Feel free to download the code used from this book's GitHub site at https://github.com/jfdimarzio/AndroidStudioGameDev.

Index

A, B

Android Studio
  code editor, 21–23
  installation, 3, 5
  interface, 19
  JDK, 1, 3
  layout editor, 23–24
  project window, 19, 21
  updating, 5–6, 8

C, D, E

Code editor, 21–23
Collision detection
  if statement, 86
  jump method, 85–86
  onTouchEvent(), 85–86
  OpenGL ES, 86
  robust collision (*see* Robust
    collision detection)

F

Fragment shaders, 45

G, H

Game development
  3D, 39
  android games, 39
  android SDKs, 39

game engine, 40
game loop, 41
Java, 40
Game engine, 40
Game loop, 41
Game movement
  GameRenderer class, 81–82
  Hero class, 81
  heroMove float, 82–83
  onTouchEvent(), 82
Gesture listener, 77, 79–80
Getter and setter code, 25
GitHub
  account settings, 31–33
  Git, 29
  installation wizard, 30
  master password set up, 34
  Use Git selection, 30–31
  VCS
    Enable Version Control
     Integration, 35
    GitHub selection window, 33
    repository naming and
     description, 37
    Share project on GitHub, 36
GLSL. *See* OpenGL Shading
    Language (GLSL)
GlSurfaceView, 47
GLSurfaceView.Renderer, 47
Graphics processing
    unit (GPU), 44

Get the eBook for only $5!

Why limit yourself?

Now you can take the weightless companion with you wherever you go and access your content on your PC, phone, tablet, or reader.

Since you've purchased this print book, we're happy to offer you the eBook in all 3 formats for just $5.

Convenient and fully searchable, the PDF version enables you to easily find and copy code—or perform examples by quickly toggling between instructions and applications. The MOBI format is ideal for your Kindle, while the ePUB can be utilized on a variety of mobile devices.

To learn more, go to www.apress.com/companion or contact support@apress.com.

Printed in the United States
By Bookmasters